Childcraft
The How and Why Library

Volume 2

Stories and Fables

World Book–Childcraft International, Inc.

A subsidiary of The Scott & Fetzer Company

Chicago London Sydney Tokyo Toronto

Acknowledgments

The publishers of *Childcraft—The How and Why Library*
gratefully acknowledge the courtesy of the following
publishers and authors for permission to use copyrighted
stories and illustrations. Full illustration acknowledgments
for this volume appear on page 302.

Coward-McCann, Inc.: *The Five Chinese Brothers* by
Claire Huchet Bishop and Kurt Wiese; "Feboldson,
Western Scientist" from *Tall Tale America* by Walter
Blair, copyright 1944 by Walter Blair; *Gone Is Gone* by
Wanda Gág, copyright 1935 by Wanda Gág, courtesy
Faber and Faber, Ltd.; *The Story of Kattor* by Georgia
Travers, copyright 1939 by Georgia Travers and Flavia
Gág

Crowell Company, Thomas Y.: "Anansi and the Plantains"
from *Anansi the Spider Man* by Philip M. Sherlock,
copyright 1954 by Philip M. Sherlock

The Dial Press, Inc.: "The Flight of Icarus" reprinted
from *Stories of the Gods and Heroes* by Sally Benson.
Copyright 1940 by Sally Benson and used by permission
of the publisher, The Dial Press, Inc.

Doubleday & Company, Inc.: *Shawneen and the Gander*
by Richard Bennett, copyright 1937 by Richard Bennett;
"The Poppy Seed Cakes" from *The Poppy Seed Cakes*
by Margery Clark, copyright 1924 by Doubleday &
Company, Inc.; "How the Camel Got His Hump" from
Just So Stories by Rudyard Kipling, copyright 1912,
1897 by Rudyard Kipling, courtesy Mrs. George
Bambridge, Macmillan Company of Canada, Ltd.; and
Messrs. Macmillan and Company, Ltd.

Dutton & Co., Inc., E. P.: "In Which Pooh Goes Visiting
and Gets Into a Tight Place" from the book *Winnie-the-
Pooh* by A. A. Milne, illustrated by E. H. Shephard,
copyright 1926 by E. P. Dutton & Co., Inc., renewal 1954
by A. A. Milne, reprinted by permission of the publishers
and Methuen & Co. Ltd.; "The Turnip" from *Russian
Tales for Children* by Alexei Tolstoi, courtesy Routledge
& Kegan Paul, Ltd.

Harcourt, Brace and Company, Inc.: "How They Bring
Back the Village of Cream Puffs When the Wind Blows
It Away" from *Rootabaga Stories* by Carl Sandburg,

copyright 1922, 1923 by Harcourt, Brace and Company,
Inc., renewed 1950, 1951 by Carl Sandburg; "The Old
Man with the Bump" from *The Dancing Kettle and Other
Japanese Folk Tales*, retold by Yoshiko Uchida, copy-
right 1949 by Yoshiko Uchida

Harper & Brothers: "The Skunk in Tante Odette's Oven"
from *The Talking Cat* by Natalie Savage Carlson,
copyright 1952 by Natalie Savage Carlson

Hercules Incorporated: illustration, pages 292, 295, and
Heritage binding cover, copyright 1959 by Hercules
Incorporated

Houghton Mifflin Company: *The Fast Sooner Hound* by
Arna Bontemps and Jack Conroy

Lofting, Hugh, The Estate of: "Dr. Dolittle's Pushmi-
Pullyu" from *The Story of Dr. Dolittle* by Hugh Lofting

McKay Company, Inc., David: "How It Snowed Fur and
Rained Fry Cakes in Western Virginia" from *The
Remarkable History of Tony Beaver—West Virginian*
by Mary E. Cober, copyright 1953 by Mary E. Cober

Nelson & Sons, Thomas: "How She Kept Her Geese
Warm" from *The Little Old Woman Who Used Her Head*
by Hope Newell

Putnam's Sons, G. P.: "The Little Red Hen and the Grain
of Wheat" from *Chimney Corner Stories*, edited by
Veronica S. Hutchinson; *Little Toot* by Hardie Gramatky,
copyright 1939 by Hardie Gramatky

Row, Peterson & Company: "Gudbrand-on-the-Hillside"
and "Three Billy Goats Gruff" from *East o' the Sun
and West o' the Moon*, retold by Gudrun Thorne-Thomsen,
copyright 1946 by Row, Peterson & Company

Time Inc.: photography by George Silk, page 61, courtesy
Life magazine, copyright 1961 by Time Inc.

The Viking Press, Inc.: "Ice" from *The Tough Winter*
by Robert Lawson, copyright 1954 by Robert Lawson;
"Why the Kangaroo Hops on Two Legs," an adaptation
of the story "Bohra the Kangaroo" from *Australian
Legendary Tales* by K. Langloh Parker, selected by
H. Drake-Brockman, all rights reserved, reprinted
by permission of The Viking Press, Inc., and Angus
and Robertson, Publishers

Volume 2

Stories and Fables

Contents

ANIMAL TALES

Goldilocks and the Three Bears

Once upon a time there were three Bears who lived in a little house in the woods. There was a Great Big Father Bear, with a great big voice, and a Middle-Sized Mother Bear, with a middle-sized voice, and a Little Wee Baby Bear, with a little, wee voice.

One morning the three Bears had porridge for breakfast, and the Mother Bear said,

"This porridge is too hot to eat now. Let us go to the woods for a walk, while the porridge gets cold."

So the three Bears went for a walk in the woods.

Now while they were gone, along came a little girl named Goldilocks. When she saw the little house in the woods she wondered who lived there, so she knocked at the door. No one answered, so she knocked again. Still no one answered, so Goldilocks opened the door and walked in.

There before her, in the little room, she saw a table set for three. There was a great big bowl of porridge, a middle-sized bowl of porridge, and a little, wee bowl of porridge. She tasted the great big bowl of porridge.

"Oh, this is too hot!" she said.

Then she tasted the middle-sized bowl of porridge.

"Oh, this is too cold!"

Then she tasted the little, wee bowl of porridge.

"Oh, this is just right!" she said, and ate it all up.

Then she went into another room, and there she saw three chairs. There was a great big chair and a middle-sized chair and a little, wee chair. Goldilocks sat down in the great big chair.

"Oh, this is too hard!" she said.

Then she sat down in the middle-sized chair.

"Oh, this is too soft!"

Then she sat in the little, wee chair.

"Oh, this is just right!" and she sat down so hard that she sat the bottom out.

Then she went into another room, and there she saw three beds. There was a great big bed and a middle-sized bed and a little, wee bed. Goldilocks lay down on the great big bed.

"Oh, this is too hard!" she said.

Then she tried the middle-sized bed.

"Oh, this is too soft!"

Then she tried the little, wee bed.

"Oh, this is just right!" she sighed, and fell fast asleep.

Now while Goldilocks was asleep, the three Bears returned from their walk in the woods. They looked at the table, and the Great Big Father Bear said, in his great big voice,

"SOMEONE HAS BEEN TASTING MY PORRIDGE."

The Middle-Sized Mother Bear said, in her middle-sized voice,

"SOMEONE HAS BEEN TASTING MY PORRIDGE."

And the Little Wee Baby Bear said, in his little, wee voice,

"*Someone has been tasting my porridge and has eaten it all up!*"

Then the three Bears went into the next room. The Great Big Father Bear looked at his chair and said, in his great big voice,

"SOMEONE HAS BEEN SITTING IN MY CHAIR."

Then the Middle-Sized Mother Bear said in her middle-sized voice,

"SOMEONE HAS BEEN SITTING IN MY CHAIR."

And the Little Wee Baby Bear cried, in his little, wee voice,

"*Someone has been sitting in my chair, and has sat the bottom out!*"

Then the three Bears went into their bedroom. The Great Big Father Bear said, in his great big voice,

"SOMEONE HAS BEEN LYING IN MY BED."

And the Middle-Sized Mother Bear said, in her middle-sized voice,

"SOMEONE HAS BEEN LYING IN MY BED."

And the Little Wee Baby Bear cried, in his little, wee voice,

"Someone has been lying in my bed, and here she is!"

Now the shrill voice of the Little Wee Baby Bear waked Goldilocks, and you may well believe she was frightened to see the three Bears looking at her. She jumped from the bed, ran across the room, sprang out of the little, low window, and away she ran through the woods as fast as ever her legs could carry her.

The Three Little Pigs

Once upon a time there was a Mother Pig with three Little Pigs. As she did not have enough money to keep them, she sent them out to seek their fortune.

The first Little Pig met a Man with a bundle of straw and said to him, "Please, Man, give me that straw to build a house." The Man did, and the Little Pig built a house of straw.

Presently, a Wolf came along and knocked at the door. The Wolf said, "Little Pig, Little Pig, let me come in."

To which the Little Pig answered, "No, no, not by the hair on my chinny chin chin."

"Then I'll huff and I'll puff, and I'll blow your house in!" said the Wolf. So he huffed and he puffed, and he blew the house in, and ate up the Little Pig.

The second Little Pig met a Man with a bundle of sticks and said, "Please, Man, give me those sticks to

build a house." The Man did, and the Little Pig built a house of sticks.

Then along came the Wolf and said, "Little Pig, Little Pig, let me come in."

"No, no, not by the hair on my chinny chin chin," said the second Little Pig.

"Then I'll puff and I'll huff, and I'll blow your house in!" said the Wolf. So he huffed and he puffed, and he puffed and he huffed, and at last he blew the house down, and ate up the second Little Pig.

The third Little Pig met a Man with a load of bricks, and said, "Please, Man, give me those bricks to build a house." The Man did, and the third Little Pig built a house of bricks.

Then the Wolf came along and said, as he had to the other Little Pigs, "Little Pig, Little Pig, let me come in."

"No, no, not by the hair on my chinny chin chin," said the third Little Pig.

"Then I'll huff and I'll puff, and I'll blow your house in," cried the Wolf. Well, he huffed and he puffed, and he puffed and he huffed, and he huffed and he puffed. But he could not blow the house down. When he found that he could not, with all his huffing and puffing, blow

the house down, he said, "Little Pig, I know where there is a nice field of turnips."

"Where?" asked the Little Pig.

"Oh, in Mr. Smith's field. If you will be ready tomorrow morning, I will call for you, and we will go together and get some for dinner."

"Very well," said the Little Pig, "I'll be ready. What time do you mean to go?"

"At six o'clock," said the Wolf.

Well, the Little Pig got up at five, got the turnips, and was home again before six. When the Wolf came he said, "Little Pig, are you ready?"

"*Ready?*" asked the Little Pig. "I have been and come back again. I have a nice potful of turnips for dinner."

The Wolf was very angry, but he still thought he could trick the Little Pig somehow or other. So he said, "Little Pig, I know where there is a nice apple tree."

"Where?" asked the Little Pig.

"Down at Merry-Garden," replied the Wolf. "If you promise not to fool me, I will come for you at five o'clock tomorrow and we will get some apples."

Well, the Little Pig woke at four the next morning and went off to get the apples. He hoped to be back before the Wolf came, but he had farther to go and also had to climb the tree. Just as he was coming down from the tree, he saw the Wolf coming. As you may suppose, that frightened him very much.

When the Wolf came up he said, "Little Pig, what are you doing here before me? Are they nice apples?"

"Yes, very," said the Little Pig; "I will throw you down one." And he threw it as far as he could. While the Wolf was gone to pick it up, the Little Pig jumped down and ran home.

The next day the Wolf came again, and said to the Little Pig, "Little Pig, there is a Fair in the town this afternoon. Will you go?"

"Oh, yes," said the Little Pig, "I'll go. What time will you be ready?"

"At three," said the Wolf.

So the Little Pig went off early, as usual, got to the Fair, bought a butter churn, and was on his way home with it when he saw the Wolf coming. At first he did not know what to do. He got into the butter churn to hide. In doing so, he turned it round so that it began to roll. And it rolled down the hill with the Little Pig inside it. The Wolf was

so frightened by this that he ran home without going to the Fair.

Later, the Wolf went to the Little Pig's house and told him how frightened he had been by a great round thing which came down the hill past him.

Then the Little Pig said, "Hah! I frightened you, did I? I had been to the Fair and bought a butter churn. When I saw you, I got into it and rolled down the hill."

Then the Wolf was very angry indeed. He declared he *would* eat up the Little Pig, and that he would climb down the chimney after him.

When the Little Pig saw what the Wolf was about, he put a pot full of water in the fireplace and made a blazing fire. Just as the Wolf was coming down the chimney, the Little Pig took the cover off the pot and in fell the Wolf! The Little Pig put the cover on again, instantly boiled up the Wolf, ate him for supper, and lived happily ever after.

The Monkey and the Crocodile

Retold by Ellen C. Babbitt

A Monkey lived in a great tree on a riverbank. In the river there were many Crocodiles.

A Crocodile watched the Monkeys for a long time, and one day she said to her son: "My son, get one of those Monkeys for me. I want the heart of a Monkey to eat."

"How am I to catch a Monkey?" asked the little Crocodile. "I do not travel on land, and the Monkey does not go into the water."

"Put your wits to work, and you'll find a way," said the mother.

And the little Crocodile thought and thought.

At last he said to himself: "I know what I'll do. I'll get that Monkey that lives in a big tree on the riverbank. He wishes to go across the river to the island where the fruit is so ripe."

So the Crocodile swam to the tree where the Monkey lived. But he was a stupid Crocodile.

"Oh, Monkey," he called, "come with me over to the island where the fruit is so ripe."

"How can I go with you?" asked the Monkey. "I do not swim."

"No—but I do. I will take you over on my back," said the Crocodile.

The Monkey was greedy, and wanted the ripe fruit, so he jumped down on the Crocodile's back.

"Off we go!" said the Crocodile.

"This is a fine ride you are giving me!" said the Monkey.

"Do you think so? Well, how do you like this?" asked the Crocodile, diving.

"Oh, don't!" cried the Monkey, as he went under the water. He was afraid to let go, and he did not know what to do under the water.

When the Crocodile came up, the Monkey sputtered and choked. "Why did you take me underwater, Crocodile?" he asked.

"I am going to kill you by keeping you underwater," answered the Crocodile. "My mother wants Monkey-heart to eat, and I'm going to take yours to her."

"I wish you had told me you wanted my heart," said the Monkey, "then I might have brought it with me."

"How queer!" said the stupid Crocodile. "Do you mean to say that you left your heart back there in the tree?"

"That is what I mean," said the Monkey. "If you want

my heart, we must go back to the tree and get it. But we are so near the island where the ripe fruit is, please take me there first."

"No, Monkey," said the Crocodile, "I'll take you straight back to your tree. Never mind the ripe fruit. Get your heart and bring it to me at once. Then we'll see about going to the island."

"Very well," said the Monkey.

But no sooner had he jumped onto the bank of the river than—whisk! up he ran into the tree.

From the topmost branches he called down to the Crocodile in the water below:

"My heart is way up here! If you want it, come for it, come for it!"

Dr. Dolittle's Pushmi-Pullyu

by Hugh Lofting

Dr. Dolittle loved animals so much that he decided, instead of doctoring people, he would be an animal doctor. On the advice of Chee-Chee, his pet monkey, he made the long voyage to Africa to cure the monkeys there of a strange disease. That done, he told the monkeys that he must go back to his home in Puddleby.

They were very surprised at this; for they had thought that he was going to stay with them forever. And that night all the monkeys got together in the jungle to talk it over.

And the Chief Chimpanzee rose up and said, "Why is it the good man is going away? Is he not happy here with us?"

But none of them could answer him.

Then the Grand Gorilla got up and said, "I think we all should go to him and ask him to stay. Perhaps if we make him a new house and a bigger bed, and promise him plenty of monkey-servants to work for him and to make life pleasant for him—perhaps then he will not wish to go."

Then Chee-Chee got up; and all the others whispered, "Sh! Look! Chee-Chee, the great Traveler, is about to speak!"

And Chee-Chee said to the other monkeys, "My friends, I am afraid it is useless to ask the Doctor to stay. He owes money in Puddleby; and he says he must go back and pay it."

And the monkeys asked him, "What is *money?*"

Then Chee-Chee told them that in the Land of the White Men you could get nothing without money; you could *do* nothing without money—that it was almost impossible to *live* without money.

And some of them asked, "But can you not even eat and drink without paying?"

Chee-Chee shook his head. And then he told them that even he, when he was with the organ-grinder, had been made to ask the children for money.

And the Chief Chimpanzee turned to the Oldest Orangoutang and said, "Cousin, surely these Men be strange creatures! Who would wish to live in such a land? My gracious, how paltry!"

Then Chee-Chee said, "When we were coming to you we had no boat to cross the sea in and no money to buy food to eat on our journey. So a man lent us some biscuits; and we said we would pay him when we came back. And we borrowed a boat from a sailor; but it was broken on the rocks when we reached the shores of Africa. Now the Doctor says he must go back and get the sailor another boat—because the man was poor and his ship was all he had."

And the monkeys were all silent for a while, sitting quite still upon the ground and thinking hard.

At last the Biggest Baboon got up and said, "I do not think we ought to let this good man leave our land till we have given him a fine present to take with him, so that he may know we are grateful for all that he has done for us."

And a little, tiny red monkey who was sitting up in a tree shouted down, "I think that, too!"

And then they all cried out, making a great noise, "Yes, yes. Let us give him the finest present a White Man ever had!"

Now they began to wonder and ask one another what would be the best thing to give him. And one said, "Fifty bags of coconuts!" And another, "A hundred bunches of bananas! At least he shall not have to buy his fruit in the Land Where You Pay to Eat!"

But Chee-Chee told them that all these things would be too heavy to carry so far and would go bad before half was eaten.

"If you want to please him," he said, "give him an animal. You may be sure he will be kind to it. Give him some rare animal they have not got in the menageries."

And the monkeys asked him, "What are *menageries?*"

Then Chee-Chee explained to them that menageries were places in the Land of the White Men, where animals were put in cages for people to come and look at. And the monkeys were very shocked and said to one another,

"These Men are like thoughtless young ones—stupid and easily amused. Sh! It is a prison he means."

So then they asked Chee-Chee what rare animal it could be that they should give the Doctor—one the White Men had not seen before. And the Major of the Marmosettes asked,

"Have they an iguana over there?"

But Chee-Chee said, "Yes, there is one in the London Zoo."

And another asked, "Have they an okapi?"

But Chee-Chee said, "Yes. In Belgium where my organ-grinder took me five years ago, they had an okapi in a big city they call Antwerp."

And another asked, "Have they a pushmi-pullyu?"

Then Chee-Chee said, "No. No White Man has ever seen a pushmi-pullyu. Let us give him that."

Pushmi-pullyus are now extinct. That means, there aren't any more. But long ago, when Doctor Dolittle was alive, there were some of them still left in the deepest jungles of Africa; and even then they were very, very scarce. They had no tail, but a head at each end, and sharp horns on each head. They were very shy and terribly hard to catch. The black men get most of their animals by sneaking up behind them while they are not looking. But you could not do this with the pushmi-pullyu—because, no matter which way you came towards him, he was always facing you. And besides, only one half of him slept at a time. The other head was always awake—and watching. This was why they were never caught and never seen in zoos. Though many of the greatest huntsmen and the cleverest menagerie-keepers spent years of their lives searching through the jungles in all weathers for pushmi-pullyus, not a single one had ever been caught. Even then, years ago, he was the only animal in the world with two heads.

Well, the monkeys set out hunting for this animal through the forest. And after they had gone a good many miles, one of them found peculiar footprints near the edge of a river; and they knew that a pushmi-pullyu must be very near that spot.

Then they went along the bank of the river a little way and they saw a place where the grass was high and thick; and they guessed that he was in there.

So they all joined hands and made a great circle round the high grass. The pushmi-pullyu heard them coming; and he tried hard to break through the ring of monkeys. But he couldn't do

D'APRÈS LOFTING

it. When he saw that it was no use trying to escape, he sat down and waited to see what they wanted.

They asked him if he would go with Doctor Dolittle and be put on show in the Land of the White Men.

But he shook both his heads hard and said, "Certainly not!"

They explained to him that he would not be shut up in a menagerie but would just be looked at. They told him that the Doctor was a very kind man but hadn't any money; and people would pay to see a two-headed animal and the Doctor would get rich and could pay for the boat he had borrowed to come to Africa in.

But he answered, "No. You know how shy I am—I hate being stared at." And he almost began to cry.

Then for three days they tried to persuade him.

And at the end of the third day he said he would come with them and see what kind of a man the Doctor was, first.

So the monkeys traveled back with the pushmi-pullyu. And when they came to where the Doctor's little house of grass was, they knocked on the door.

The duck, who was packing the trunk, said, "Come in!"

And Chee-Chee very proudly took the animal inside and showed him to the Doctor.

"What in the world is it?" asked John Dolittle, gazing at the strange creature.

D'APRÈS LOFTING

"Lord save us!" cried the duck. "How does it make up its mind?"

"It doesn't look to me as though it had any," said Jip, the dog.

"This, Doctor," said Chee-Chee, "is the pushmi-pullyu—the rarest animal of the African jungles, the only two-headed beast in the world! Take him home with you and your fortune's made. People will pay any money to see him."

"But I don't want any money," said the Doctor.

"Yes, you do," said Dab-Dab, the duck. "Don't you remember how we had to pinch and scrape to pay the butcher's bill in Puddleby? And how are you going to get the sailor the new boat you spoke of—unless we have the money to buy it?"

"I was going to make him one," said the Doctor.

"Oh, do be sensible!" cried Dab-Dab. "Where would you get all the wood and the nails to make one with?—And besides, what are we going to live on? We shall be poorer than ever when we get back. Chee-Chee's perfectly right; take the funny-looking thing along, do!"

"Well, perhaps there is something in what you say," murmured the Doctor. "It certainly would make a nice new kind of pet. But does the er—what-do-you-call-it really want to go abroad?"

"Yes, I'll go," said the pushmi-pullyu who saw at once, from the Doctor's face, that he was a man to be trusted. "You have been so kind to the animals here—and the monkeys tell me that I am the only one who will do. But you must promise me that if I do not like it in the Land of the White Men you will send me back."

"Why, certainly—of course, of course," said the Doctor. "Excuse me, surely you are related to the Deer Family, are you not?"

"Yes," said the pushmi-pullyu—"to the Abyssinian Gazelles and the Asiatic Chamois—on my mother's side. My father's great-grandfather was the last of the Unicorns."

"Most interesting!" murmured the Doctor; and he took a book out of the trunk which Dab-Dab was packing and began turning the pages. "Let us see if Buffon says anything—"

"I notice," said the duck, "that you only talk with one of your mouths. Can't the other head talk as well?"

"Oh, yes," said the pushmi-pullyu. "But I keep the other mouth for eating—mostly. In that way I can talk while I am eating without being rude. Our people have always been very polite."

When the packing was finished and everything was ready to start, the monkeys gave a grand party for the Doctor, and all the animals of the jungle came. And they had pineapples and mangoes and honey and all sorts of good things to eat and drink.

After they had all finished eating, the Doctor got up and said, "My friends: I am not clever at speaking long words after dinner, like some men; and I have just eaten many fruits and much honey. But I wish to tell you that I am very sad at leaving your beautiful country. Because I have things to do in the Land of the White Men, I must go. After I have gone, remember never to let the flies settle on your food before you eat it; and do not sleep on the ground when the rains are coming. I—er—er—I hope you will all live happily ever after."

When the Doctor stopped speaking and sat down, all the monkeys clapped their hands a long time and said to one another, "Let it be remembered always among our people that· he sat and ate with us, here, under the trees. For surely he is the Greatest of Men!"

And the Grand Gorilla, who had the strength of seven horses in his hairy arms, rolled a great rock up to the head of the table and said,

"This stone for all time shall mark the spot."

And even to this day, in the heart of the jungle, that stone still is there. And monkey-mothers, passing through the forest with their families, still point down at it from the branches and whisper to their children, "Sh! There it is—look—where the Good White Man sat and ate food with us in the Year of the Great Sickness!"

Then, when the party was over, the Doctor and his pets started out to go back to the seashore. And all the monkeys went with him as far as the edge of their country, carrying his trunk and bags, to see him off.

D'APRÈS LOFTING

ICE

Story and Pictures by Robert Lawson

All through the night it snowed heavily. In the morning Uncle Analdas, always the first up, went to the burrow entrance, butted and kicked his way out through the now deep snow, came back, shook himself well, and climbed into bed again. "A good foot, now," he said gloomily, pulling the blankets up around his chin, "and still a-comin'." In a few minutes he was snoring peacefully.

About noon there was a slight difference in the sound of the softly falling snow, and Father went out to observe. "Rain," he reported. "A freezing rain. There is a considerable crust on the snow. I had some difficulty in breaking out."

Little Georgie had slept as much as he could and was becoming extremely bored when, late in the afternoon, they were all roused by a sudden commotion at the burrow entrance. In burst Willie Fieldmouse, followed by three of his young cousins. The young cousins, fairly well blown by their tunneling efforts, at once settled themselves by the fireplace. Willie, however, was bursting with excitement.

"Oh, Georgie," he cried, "the old Cat is lost—Mr. Muldoon, you know. The Folks were calling him all night, and the Man has been tramping around the fields all day in this freezing rain and he can't find him. But I know where he is. I found him, but I can't do anything about it."

"You are somewhat overexcited, William," Father said, "and your account lacks coherence. You say the Cat is lost but you have found him. Therefore he cannot be lost. Now suppose you sit down and tell us quietly just what has happened."

"Yessir, I'll try," Willie answered. "Well, we were digging a tunnel to Uncle Sleeper's—he lives down along the wall there, and Mother wanted to be sure he was all right—and suddenly we came on the old Cat holed up under the snow right beside the wall. He must have gotten lost, and when the snow got too deep he just got in a little hole there by the wall and let it snow over him and kept turning around until he had a nice little room all hollowed out. And now he can't get out because there's an awful thick crust on top of the snow."

"The poor old thing!" Mother said. "Isn't he terribly cold, Willie?"

"No, ma'am, I don't think so," replied Willie. "Of course I didn't *feel* him, but it's nice and warm there under the snow.

He must be getting real hungry though. That's why we didn't stay around very long."

"The poor Folks!" Mother exclaimed. "And them getting ready to go away and all and the Cat lost and them so fond of him! It does seem to me there ought to be something we could do and him so nice to all of us and never harmed a soul. Oh, Analdas, isn't there *something* you and Father and Georgie could do?"

"Not me," Uncle Analdas answered promptly. "It's agin Nature, that's what it is. Since when have Mice and Rabbits taken to helpin' out Cats? Maybe he ain't ever done nothin' *to* any of us, but he ain't ever done nothin' *fer* any of us neither. Nossir, I ain't one to fly in the face of Nature." He pulled up the blankets and went to sleep again.

"Foxy had a lovely turkey carcass last night," Little Georgie said thoughtfully. "There was a lot of nice meat on it. If we could only get some of that to Mr. Muldoon he'd at least have something to eat, but I guess we can't. Foxy's iced in just like the rest of us."

"I think maybe we can. I know we can," squeaked Willie Fieldmouse excitedly. He sat quiet for a time, and they could see him going over in his mind all the maze of Mouse tunnels that covered the Hill. "Look," he finally said, "there's a tunnel from here to our place, and then there's one that goes up through the rock garden to Aunt Minnie's—Father dug that one this morning. Then from there there's a long one up to Uncle Stackpole's, way up near the Pine Wood, I'm sure that's dug by now. Foxy's den is right close to that one, I know exactly where. It'll only take us a little while to dig in to him. Then, if he'll let us have a little turkey meat, we can drag it down and give it to Mr. Muldoon."

"I wonder if he will," Little Georgie said doubtfully. "Foxy doesn't know Mr. Muldoon very well, and I don't think he cares especially about him one way or the other."

"You will have to be most diplomatic and persuasive, William," Father instructed. "Be very polite and use all the powers of eloquence at your command. You might mention that compliance with your request would bring deep pleasure to Mother and me."

"Yessir," replied Willie. "Come on, boys." The three young

cousins rose from the fireplace somewhat reluctantly, shook themselves, and scampered up the tunnel.

"It may take some time," Willie called back, "but we'll do our best."

Mother, Father, and Little Georgie sat through the long evening in silence, their minds filled with thoughts of the old Cat trapped in his tiny refuge under the icy crust. Mother's thoughts turned mostly to the Folks and their distress. Uncle Analdas snored.

The freezing rain seemed to have stopped, but the wind had risen. Every now and then they could hear the jar and crash of some great ice-coated tree branch falling to earth. Although outside sounds were muffled they could recognize the roar and clatter of trucks plowing the Black Road, could sometimes hear the shouts of linemen battling to repair fallen wires. Finally Little Georgie dozed off.

He was wakened by a cry from Mother and the excited chittering of Fieldmice. There stood Willie and his three cousins, each dragging a long sliver of plump white turkey meat. They were thoroughly exhausted, and Mother insisted that they take a short rest before finishing their journey.

"Well, William," Father congratulated him, "I am delighted to see that your good manners and eloquence prevailed on Foxy. I trust that the mention of my name was also of some assistance."

"He was asleep," Willie said grinning. "So we didn't have to be eloquent. We had to be awful quiet though—that's why it took so long."

They resumed their burdens and set off toward Mr. Muldoon's refuge. They were soon back. "He just loved it," Willie reported. "He gobbled up every piece as fast as we could push it in. But we didn't stay around long. He might still have been a *little* hungry."

Next morning Little Georgie was waked by the voices of Father and Uncle Analdas. Evidently they had been up some time, for they had clawed an opening up through the snow as far as the icy top crust. There they were stopped. All their pushing and grunting, thumping and kicking, were to no avail.

"Mebbe the sun'll soften the dingblasted ice," Uncle Analdas growled. "*Now* who was right about a tough winter, and it hardly begun yet!" He went back to bed.

Little Georgie went out and stared up at the icy sheet that imprisoned them. It looked like frosted glass, with the sun glimmering through it. Apparently the wind was blowing strongly, for he could hear twigs and branches sliding and skittering over the surface. He wished he could tunnel under the snow as skillfully as Willie Fieldmouse, and tried it, but he didn't get very far. Then they had breakfast and waited for Uncle Analdas to wake up.

When he did, an hour or two later, they went out to try again. As Father and Uncle Analdas pushed and grunted the crust *did* seem to be giving slightly. Little Georgie clambered up on their shoulders and heaved and pushed as hard as he could.

With a great cracking the ice crust suddenly gave way and Little Georgie was shot out into the blinding sunlight.

He was speechless with surprise at the way the looks of things had changed. Fallen branches, large and small, lay everywhere. Shrubs were flattened. Slender saplings were bent over like croquet wickets. The tall cedars were splayed out like worn-out brushes. And every twig, every boulder, even the red brick house, was sheathed in winking, glittering ice. The wind was bitterly cold, but the sun had begun to loosen the ice, which was now falling from the trees in tinkling showers.

He could see the Man and Tim McGrath attacking the fallen boughs with saws and axes, carefully searching under each one.

Uncle Analdas shook the snow out of his ears and went off to see if any of the other Animals had managed to break out. Father and Little Georgie hastened along the wall to the spot beyond the little oak tree where Willie Fieldmouse had said Mr. Muldoon was buried. They found the place easily, but though they rapped and scratched no sound came from below the ice. Mr. Muldoon's plight seemed pretty hopeless.

Suddenly Little Georgie had an idea, and without a word to Father he dashed off up the Hill. It was rather tough going, for the icy crust was terribly slippery and the wind was strong. He had a great many slips and tumbles before reaching the shelter of the Pine Wood.

Here the ice had hardly penetrated; the snow was still soft and fluffy. He floundered and hopped through it until he saw the warm brown form of the Red Buck. The Buck had tramped down the snow in a neat circular yard and was quietly browsing on hemlock twigs.

"Good morning sir, and good luck to you," Little Georgie said politely.

"Good morning, Georgie," replied the Buck, "and how have all you little fellows fared in the storm?"

"Not very well, sir," Georgie answered. "Most everyone's still iced in, and poor Mr. Muldoon—" He plunged into an account of Mr. Muldoon's plight, ending with a plea for the Buck's assistance.

"Well, I don't know," the Buck answered dubiously. "Hate to walk in an ice crust—cuts your ankles real nasty. Snow covers up holes and mole runs and stones too—can break a leg easy as not. I've never had much to do with that Cat; ordinarily I wouldn't bother with him. Still and all, we do owe the Folks an awful lot, and I suppose I ought to do what I can to help out. Come ahead, we'll try it anyway."

Going down the Hill, the Buck walked with extreme care, thrusting each hoof gingerly through the icy crust, feeling his footing and withdrawing his hoofs very gently. Little Georgie, in high good spirits, galloped in circles, slithered and skittered and took long breath-taking coasts on the slippery surface. Tim McGrath and the Man stopped their labors to watch quietly as the two Animals passed.

Father had been scratching and thumping at the ice but had made no impression at all, although he thought he had heard Mr. Muldoon mew once or twice.

Now the Buck, rapping on the crust with his chisel-sharp hoof, broke it up and began carefully pawing away the slabs of ice. As he worked closer and closer to the spot where Father thought the mewing had come from, Little Georgie's breath grew short with excitement.

Finally with a gentle heave the Buck pried up one last large slab, revealing Mr. Muldoon neatly curled in his snowy nest. The old Cat rose, somewhat stiffly, shook himself irritably, and without so much as a glance at his rescuers stalked away up the Hill, his dignified pace interrupted now and then by an awkward sprawl on the icy surface. Father immediately hastened back to the burrow to relieve Mother's mind.

The Man gathered the Cat in his arms and went up to the house, but Tim McGrath continued to stare in open-mouthed wonder. He watched while the Deer, with Little Georgie running gay circles around him, carefully retraced his steps up the Hill. The Buck's ankles were cut and scraped by the crust, and an occasional drop of blood marked his trail.

Tim walked down to the wall; examined the old Cat's refuge, the Deer's footprints, and the pawed away slabs of ice. "Holy Saints," he murmured, "if I hadn't seen it with me own two eyes I wouldn't've believed it! I'm not sure I do now."

He went to the toolhouse, gathered a huge armful of hay, and lugged it up the Hill to the edge of the Pine Wood, where he spread it out beside the Deer's trail. "Feedin' the wild stock!" He laughed at himself a bit sheepishly. "I must be getting soft in the head. Next thing I'll take to readin' books."

(From The Tough Winter)

THE LITTLE RED HEN AND THE GRAIN OF WHEAT

Retold by Veronica S. Hutchinson

One day the Little Red Hen
was scratching in the farmyard,
when she found a grain of wheat.
   "Who will plant the wheat?" said she.
   "Not I," said the duck.
   "Not I," said the cat.
   "Not I," said the dog.
   "Very well then,"
said the Little Red Hen, "I will."

...not I said the duck...

So she planted the grain of wheat.
After some time the wheat
grew tall and ripe.
"Who will cut the wheat?"
asked the Little Red Hen.
"Not I," said the duck.
"Not I," said the cat.
"Not I," said the dog.
"Very well then, I will,"
said the Little Red Hen.
So she cut the wheat.

"Now," she said, "who will thresh the wheat?"
"Not I," said the duck.
"Not I," said the cat.
"Not I," said the dog.
"Very well then, I will,"
said the Little Red Hen.
So she threshed the wheat.
When the wheat was threshed, she said,
"Who will take the wheat to the mill to have it
ground into flour?"
"Not I," said the duck.
"Not I," said the cat.
"Not I," said the dog.
"Very well then, I will," said the Little Red Hen.
So she took the wheat to the mill.

When the wheat was ground into flour, she said,
"Who will make this flour into bread?"
"Not I," said the duck.
"Not I," said the cat.
"Not I," said the dog.
"Very well then, I will,"
said the Little Red Hen,
and she baked a lovely loaf of bread.

Then she said,
"Who will eat the bread?"
"Oh! I will," said the duck.
"Oh! I will," said the cat.
"Oh! I will," said the dog.
"Oh, no, you won't!"
said the Little Red Hen. "I will."
And she called her chicks
and shared the bread with them.

not I said the cat................not I said the dog..........

THE STORY OF KATTOR

by Georgia Travers

Kattor was a baby tiger. He had a beautiful coat of yellow striped with black. His paws were as big as the boughs of a young tree and his tail was fine and swishy. His eyes were yellow and fierce, even for a small tiger's. He had a pink rough tongue which showed behind strong white teeth whenever he growled.

Kattor lived with his mother in a den of rocks in a hillside. Here he had a bed of dry crackly leaves. When he was very young he liked to lie there all day and to amuse himself by stretching out his big paws and by putting out the great claws which were hidden in the soft furry pads of his feet.

As he grew older his mother began taking Kattor out for exercise. Then he would jump about, turn somersaults, toss sticks into the air, and tear leaves to pieces with his sharp claws. He would strike playful blows at things with his front paws. He would pounce in fun at stones and shadows.

So Kattor lived and grew. Each day as he played out of doors he seemed to feel himself getting stronger and stronger.

Many months went by. Then one day Kattor ventured out all alone. He sharpened his claws on a great tall tree. He struck playfully at objects in his path. It was fun to crush them at a single blow. Wherever he went, all the other little creatures of the woods ran away screaming for their lives. This was very thrilling. How big and powerful he was!

That evening he went home and told his mother all he had done.

"I am a great strong tiger, am I not?" said Kattor.

"You are a strong *baby* tiger," said his mother. "But now you must sleep," and she fluffed up his bed of leaves, washed him tenderly with her great rough tongue, and purred to him softly as he went to sleep.

Every day after that Kattor went a little farther from home. Every day he sharpened his claws—and every day he dared to frighten bigger and bigger animals. And every night he would return to his mother and say as before, "Mother, I am a great strong tiger, am I not?" And every night his mother would reply, "You are a strong *baby* tiger." Then she would wash him with her great rough tongue, fluff up his bed of leaves, and purr softly to him until he went to sleep.

This went on for a long time. Then one day as he was sharpening his claws on a tree, he ripped and scratched so fiercely into the bark that he felt even stronger than he had ever felt before. That day he went to hunt for food for the first time and brought it home proudly to show his mother.

"Mother, I am a great strong tiger, am I not?" said Kattor. And that night his mother answered, "Yes, Kattor, you are getting to be a great strong tiger."

"Some day I will conquer the world for you," said Kattor.

"Do well what tigers can do, Kattor," said his mother softly. "It is all I ask." And she washed him tenderly with her great rough tongue, fluffed up his bed of leaves, and purred softly to him until he went to sleep.

As Kattor grew in strength he began to compare himself with all the other animals he saw. Soon he believed there was nothing he could not conquer.

"I will conquer the world for you, Mother," said Kattor again and again.

One morning as Kattor was about to go out for his daily exercise he noticed that it was darker than usual.

"What is it, Mother?" asked Kattor.

"It is a storm," said his mother.

And just then the storm broke in all its fury. The rain came in torrents, the heavens growled like thousands of angry tigers, and trees crashed before the door of the den.

"Who is strong enough to break down trees?" asked Kattor.

"It is the wind," said his mother.

"I will conquer the wind," said Kattor, and he rushed out into the storm.

"Go away, Wind, or I will scratch you," called Kattor.

The wind only roared louder and seemed to mock him.

"Go away, Wind," cried Kattor; but his voice was drowned by the fury of the storm.

Kattor struck again and again into the air. This was different from anything he had ever fought before. His strong paws seemed to strike nothing, and nothing fell. The wind only grew stronger and drove the rain into his eyes, and still Kattor fought, saying, "I will conquer you. I will. I will." And still the wind roared and drove rain against Kattor's body until finally he was so tired he could fight no longer.

Then, as suddenly as it had come, the storm stopped. Kattor stood still for a moment, astonished, and then ran joyfully in to see his mother.

"See, Mother, I have conquered the wind! I will conquer the world for you!"

His mother again said, "Kattor, do well the things tigers can do. Then you will always be happy." And she smoothed his fur with her great rough tongue and he slept.

When he woke up and thought of how he had driven away the rain and wind, he felt more powerful than ever.

This time he walked until he came to a great mountain.

"Get out of my way, Mountain," said Kattor.

He scratched and tore at the mountainside. His sharp claws caught in the crevices of the rocks and his paws stung with pain. It was not like the wind—it was like nothing he had tried to scratch before, but he would not give up. He scratched and scratched and tried to push the mountain with his strong head, but the mountain would not move.

And now the sun was beginning to set. It shone directly over the top of the mountain; it beat into Kattor's smarting, sand-filled eyes. Kattor could not go on, but he was determined not to be beaten. He would go home to rest and he would return in the morning, so he looked up the mountainside to where the sun shone.

"Oh, Mountain-under-the-Sun, I will conquer you in the morning," he said.

So he went home to his mother. She fed him, fluffed his bed of leaves, and with her great rough tongue she smoothed his fur and purred softly until he went to sleep.

"I *am* a great strong tiger," said Kattor as he was falling asleep, "am I not?"

"You are a strong *young* tiger," said his mother, and he slept.

The next morning he rose early to conquer the mountain. He had forgotten just where the mountain was, but he remembered that it was under the sun. Baby tiger that he was, he did not know that the evening sun (which he had seen over the mountain) was in the west, and that the morning sun (which was just rising) was in the east. So he went east instead of west.

He walked and walked and found no mountain. He walked and walked and still he found no mountain.

And then suddenly a quiver of delight ran through his yellow body from the tip of his ears to the end of his long swishy tail. He knew now! He had scared away the mountain after all. How strong and powerful he was!

He walked and walked and soon he came to more water than he had ever seen in his life before. It was the sea.

"Get out of my way, Water," said Kattor fiercely.

The water only lapped peacefully against the shore.

This made Kattor very angry. He rushed at the sea. He bit and tore and clawed at it but he could not grasp it. No matter how hard he struck at the water, it only closed peacefully over his paws as though it could not be hurt.

Kattor, who liked to be dry and warm and comfortable, became more and more angry. Fiercer and fiercer became his blows, and still it seemed that he could not conquer the water. He fought and fought. Water got into his nose and eyes, and he was very uncomfortable. Finally, after a long time he felt that he could not go on. He wanted only to go home to his bed of warm dry leaves. He felt weak, and turning his back toward the sea, he started unsteadily for home. But what was this which greeted his eyes? Vast stretches of wet sand lay before him. He, being a baby tiger, did not know that the tide had gone out. He believed that he had chased the water far out into the sea!

"I am, after all, the most powerful tiger in the whole world," thought Kattor, and ran home to tell his mother.

"Mother," he said, breathlessly, "I conquered the wind, I frightened the mountain, and now I have scared the water away. I am a great strong tiger."

"You are still young, but you are a great strong tiger," said his mother as she washed him with her great rough tongue, and

fluffed up his bed of leaves. Then she added softly as she purred him to sleep, "Tomorrow I will go with you."

And so the next day his mother went with him.

She led him up a high cliff where he had never been before. It was hard climbing, and they came to the ridge of a hill. Scarcely had Kattor put his head over the top of the hill when he felt a strong, strong breeze blowing over its edge.

"It is the wind," said Kattor's mother simply, and Kattor wondered how the wind had dared to come back. But before he was able to say anything, he saw in the distance the great mountain he thought he had frightened away.

"It is the mountain," said Kattor's mother.

Puzzled thoughts gathered in poor Kattor's mind. Hadn't he chased the mountain and the wind away? But when he wanted to ask his mother, he found that she had wandered to the far edge of the hill and seemed to be looking away off into the distance. Kattor went to his mother, and there before him lay the water he thought he had conquered.

"It is the sea," said his mother.

Kattor did not know what to think, but his mother said nothing more, and slowly felt her way back down over the rocks.

That evening his mother fluffed up his bed and smoothed his soft fur with her great rough tongue.

"Am I *not* a great strong tiger?" asked Kattor.

"Yes, Kattor, you are a great strong tiger," said his mother gently, "but it takes more than a great strong tiger to move the winds or the mountains or the sea." And she purred softly until Kattor fell asleep.

As though in a dream, he seemed to hear her add softly, "Do well what tigers can do, Kattor. Then you will always be happy."

IN WHICH Pooh Goes Visiting and Gets Into a Tight Place

By A. A. Milne

Edward Bear, known to his friends as Winnie-the-Pooh, or Pooh for short, was walking through the forest one day, humming proudly to himself. He had made up a little hum that very morning, as he was doing his Stoutness Exercises in front of the glass: *Tra-la-la, tra-la-la,* as he stretched up as high as he could go, and then *Tra-la-la, tra-la—oh, help!—la,* as he tried to reach his toes. After breakfast he had said it over and over to himself until he had learnt it off by heart, and now he was humming it right through, properly. It went like this:

> *Tra-la-la, tra-la-la,*
> *Tra-la-la, tra-la-la,*
> *Rum-tum-tiddle-um-tum.*
> *Tiddle-iddle, tiddle-iddle,*
> *Tiddle-iddle, tiddle-iddle,*
> *Rum-tum-tum-tiddle-um.*

Well, he was humming this hum to himself, and walking along gaily, wondering what everybody else was doing, and what it felt like, being somebody else, when suddenly he came to a sandy bank, and in the bank was a large hole.

"Aha!" said Pooh. (*Rum-tum-tiddle-um-tum.*) "If I know anything about anything, that hole means Rabbit," he said, "and Rabbit means Company," he said, "and Company means Food and Listening-to-Me-Humming and such like. *Rum-tum-tum-tiddle-um.*"

So he bent down, put his head into the hole, and called out: "Is anybody at home?"

There was a sudden scuffling noise from inside the hole, and then silence.

"What I said was, 'Is anybody at home?'" called out Pooh very loudly.

"No!" said a voice; and then added, "You needn't shout so loud. I heard you quite well the first time."

"Bother!" said Pooh. "Isn't there anybody here at all?"

"Nobody."

Winnie-the-Pooh took his head out of the hole, and thought for a little, and he thought to himself, "There must be somebody there, because somebody must have *said* 'Nobody.'" So he put his head back in the hole, and said:

"Hallo, Rabbit, isn't that you?"

"No," said Rabbit, in a different sort of voice this time.

"But isn't that Rabbit's voice?"

"I don't *think* so," said Rabbit. "It isn't *meant* to be."

"Oh!" said Pooh.

He took his head out of the hole, and had another think, and then he put it back, and said:

"Well, could you very kindly tell me where Rabbit is?"

"He has gone to see his friend Pooh Bear, who is a great friend of his."

"But this *is* Me!" said Bear, very much surprised.

"What sort of Me?"

"Pooh Bear."

"Are you sure?" said Rabbit, still more surprised.

"Quite, quite sure," said Pooh.

"Oh, well, then, come in."

So Pooh pushed and pushed and pushed his way through the hole, and at last he got in.

"You were quite right," said Rabbit, looking at him all over. "It *is* you. Glad to see you."

"Who did you think it was?"

"Well, I wasn't sure. You know how it is in the Forest. One can't have *anybody* coming into one's house. One has to be *careful*. What about a mouthful of something?"

Pooh always liked a little something at eleven o'clock in the morning, and he was very glad to see Rabbit getting out the plates and mugs; and when Rabbit said, "Honey or condensed milk with your bread?" he was so excited that he said, "Both," and then, so as not to seem greedy, he added, "But don't bother about the bread, please." And for a long time after that he said nothing . . . until at last, humming to himself in a rather sticky voice, he got up, shook Rabbit lovingly by the paw, and said that he must be going on.

"Must you?" said Rabbit politely.

"Well," said Pooh, "I could stay a little longer if it— if you——" and he tried very hard to look in the direction of the larder.

"As a matter of fact," said Rabbit, "I was going out myself directly."

"Oh, well, then, I'll be going on. Good-bye."

"Well, good-bye, if you're sure you won't have any more."

"*Is* there any more?" asked Pooh quickly.

Rabbit took the covers off the dishes, and said, "No, there wasn't."

"I thought not," said Pooh, nodding to himself. "Well, good-bye. I must be going on."

So he started to climb out of the hole. He pulled with his front paws, and pushed with his back paws, and in a little while his nose was out in the open again . . . and then his ears . . . and then his front paws . . . and then his shoulders . . . and then——

"Oh, help!" said Pooh. "I'd better go back."

"Oh, bother!" said Pooh. "I shall have to go on."

"I can't do either!" said Pooh. "Oh, help *and* bother!"

Now by this time Rabbit wanted to go for a walk too, and finding the front door full, he went out by the back door, and came round to Pooh, and looked at him.

"Hallo, are you stuck?" he asked.

"N-no," said Pooh carelessly. "Just resting and thinking and humming to myself."

"Here, give us a paw."

Pooh Bear stretched out a paw, and Rabbit pulled and pulled and pulled . . . .

"*Ow!*" cried Pooh. "You're hurting!"

"The fact is," said Rabbit, "you're stuck."

"It all comes," said Pooh crossly, "of not having front doors big enough."

"It all comes," said Rabbit sternly, "of eating too much. I thought at the time," said Rabbit, "only I didn't like to say anything," said Rabbit, "that one of us was eating too much," said Rabbit, "and I knew it wasn't *me*," he said. "Well, well, I shall go and fetch Christopher Robin."

Christopher Robin lived at the other end of the Forest, and when he came back with Rabbit, and saw the front half of Pooh, he said, "Silly old Bear," in such a loving voice that everybody felt quite hopeful again.

"I was just beginning to think," said Bear, sniffing slightly, "that Rabbit might never be able to use his front door again. And I should *hate* that," he said.

"So should I," said Rabbit.

"Use his front door again?" said Christopher Robin. "Of course he'll use his front door again."

"Good," said Rabbit.

"If we can't pull you out, Pooh, we might push you back."

Rabbit scratched his whiskers thoughtfully, and pointed out that, when once Pooh was pushed back, he was back, and of course nobody was more glad to see Pooh than *he* was, still there it was, some lived in trees and some lived underground, and——

"You mean I'd *never* get out?" said Pooh.

"I mean," said Rabbit, "that having got so far, it seems a pity to waste it."

Christopher Robin nodded.

"Then there's only one thing to be done," he said. "We shall have to wait for you to get thin again."

"How long does getting thin take?" asked Pooh anxiously.

"About a week, I should think."

"But I can't stay here for a *week!*"

"You can *stay* here all right, silly old Bear. It's getting you out which is so difficult."

"We'll read to you," said Rabbit cheerfully. "And I hope it won't snow," he added. "And I say, old fellow, you're taking up a good deal of room in my house—*do* you mind if I use your back legs as a towel-horse? Because, I mean, there they are—doing nothing—and it would be very convenient just to hang the towels on them."

"A week!" said Pooh gloomily. "*What about meals?*"

"I'm afraid no meals," said Christopher Robin, "because of getting thin quicker. But we *will* read to you."

Bear began to sigh, and then found he couldn't because he was so tightly stuck; and a tear rolled down his eye, as he said:

"Then would you read a Sustaining Book, such as would help

and comfort a Wedged Bear in Great Tightness?"

So for a week Christopher Robin read that sort of book at the North end of Pooh, and Rabbit hung his washing on the South end . . . and in between Bear felt himself getting slenderer and slenderer. And at the end of the week Christopher Robin said, "*Now!*"

So he took hold of Pooh's front paws and Rabbit took hold of Christopher Robin, and all Rabbit's friends and relations took hold of Rabbit, and they all pulled together. . . .

And for a long time Pooh only said "*Ow!*" . . .

And "*Oh!*" . . .

And then, all of a sudden, he said "*Pop!*" just as if a cork were coming out of a bottle.

And Christopher Robin and Rabbit and all Rabbit's friends and relations went head-over-heels backwards . . . and on the top of them came Winnie-the-Pooh—free!

So, with a nod of thanks to his friends, he went on with his walk through the forest, humming proudly to himself. But, Christopher Robin looked after him lovingly, and said to himself, "Silly old Bear!"

(From *Winnie-the-Pooh*)

THE
U G L Y
DUCKLING

BY HANS CHRISTIAN ANDERSEN

The country was very lovely just then—it was summer. The wheat was golden and the oats still green. The hay was stacked in the rich low meadows, where the stork marched about on his long red legs, chattering in Egyptian, the language his mother had taught him.

Round about the field and meadow lay great woods, in the midst of which were deep lakes. Yes, the country certainly was lovely. In the sunniest spot stood an old mansion surrounded by a deep moat, and great dock leaves grew from the walls of the house right down to the water's edge. Some of them were so tall that a small child could stand upright under them. In among the leaves it was as secluded as in the depths of a forest, and there a duck was sitting on her nest. Her ducklings were just about to be hatched, but she was quite tired of sitting, for it had lasted such a long time. Moreover, she had very few visitors, as the other ducks liked swimming about in the moat better than waddling up to sit under the dock leaves and gossip with her.

At last one egg after another began to crack. "Cheep, cheep!" they said. All the chicks had come to life and were poking their heads out.

"Quack, quack!" said the duck, and then they all quacked their hardest and looked about them on all sides among the green leaves. Their mother allowed them to look as much as they liked, for green is good for the eyes.

"How big the world is, to be sure!" said all the young ones. They now had ever so much more room to move about than when they were inside their eggshells.

"Do you imagine this is the whole world?" said the mother. "It stretches a long way on the other side of the garden, right into the parson's field, though I have never been as far as that. I suppose you are all here now?" She got up and looked about. "No, I declare I have not got you all yet! The biggest egg is still there. How long is this going to take?" she said, and settled herself on the nest again.

"Well, how are you getting on?" asked an old duck who had come to pay her a visit.

"This one egg is taking such a long time!" answered the sitting duck. "The shell will not crack. But now you must look at the others. They are the finest ducklings I have ever seen. They are all exactly like their father, the rascal! Yet he never comes to see me."

"Let me look at the egg which won't crack," said the old duck. "You may be sure that it is a turkey's egg! I was cheated like that once and I had no end of trouble and worry with the creatures, for I may tell you that they are afraid of the water. I simply could not get them into it. I quacked and snapped at them, but it all did no good. Let me see the egg! Yes, it is a turkey's egg. You just leave it alone, and teach the other children to swim."

"I will sit on it a little longer. I have sat so long already that I may as well go on till the Midsummer Fair comes round."

"Please yourself," said the old duck, and away she went.

At last the big egg cracked. "Cheep, cheep!" said the young one and tumbled out. How big and ugly he was! The duck looked at him.

"That is a monstrous big duckling," she said. "None of the others looked like that. Can he be a turkey chick? Well, we shall soon find that out. Into the water he shall go, if I have to kick him in myself."

The next day was gloriously fine, and the sun shone on all the green dock leaves. The mother duck with her whole family went down to the moat.

Splash! Into the water she sprang. "Quack, quack," she said, and one duckling after another plumped in. The water dashed over their heads, but they came up again and floated beautifully. Their legs went of themselves, and they were all there. Even the big ugly gray one swam about with them.

"No, that is no turkey," she said. "See how beautifully he uses his legs and how erect he holds himself. He is my own chick, after all, and not bad looking when you come to look at him properly. Quack, quack! Now come with me and I will take you out into the world and introduce you to the duckyard. But keep close to me all the time, so that no one may tread upon you. And beware of the cat!"

Then they went into the duckyard. There was a fearful uproar going on, for two broods were fighting for the head of an eel, and in the end the cat captured it.

"That's how things go in this world," said the mother duck, and she licked her bill, because she wanted to have the eel's head herself.

"Use your legs," said she. "Mind you quack properly, and bend your necks to the old duck over there. She is the grandest of us all. She has Spanish blood in her veins and that accounts for her size. And do you see? She has a red rag round her leg. That is a wonderfully fine thing, and the most extraordinary mark of distinction any duck can have. It shows clearly that she is not to be parted with, and that she is worthy of recognition both by beasts and men! Quack, now! Don't turn your toes in! A well-brought-up duckling keeps his legs wide apart just like father and mother. That's it. Now bend your necks and say quack!"

They did as they were bid, but the other ducks round about looked at them and said, quite loudly, "Just look there! Now we are to have that tribe, just as if there were not enough of us already. And, oh dear, how ugly that duckling is! We won't stand him." And a duck flew at him at once and bit him in the neck.

"Let him be," said the mother. "He is doing no harm."

"Very likely not," said the biter. "But he is so ungainly and queer that he must be whacked."

"Those are handsome children mother has," said the old duck with the rag round her leg. "They are all good looking except this one. He is not a good specimen. It's a pity you can't make him over again."

"That can't be done, your grace," said the mother duck. "He is not handsome, but he is a thoroughly good creature, and he swims as beautifully as any of the others. I think I might venture even to add that I think he will improve as he goes on, or perhaps in time he may grow smaller. He was too long in the egg, and so he has not come out with a very good figure." And then she patted his neck and stroked him down.

"The other ducklings are very pretty," said the old duck. "Now make yourselves quite at home, and if you find the head of an eel you may bring it to me."

After that they felt quite at home. But the poor duckling which had been the last to come out of the shell, and who was so ugly, was bitten, pushed about, and made fun of by both the ducks and the hens. "He is too big," they all said. The poor duckling was at his wit's end, and did not know which way to turn. He was in despair because he was so ugly and the butt of the whole duckyard.

So the first day passed, and afterwards matters grew worse and worse. The poor duckling was chased and hustled by all of them. Even his brothers and sisters ill-used him. They were always saying, "If only the cat would get hold of you, you hideous object!" Even his mother said, "I wish to goodness you were miles away." The ducks bit him, the hens pecked him, and the girl who fed them kicked him aside.

Then he ran off and flew right over the hedge, where the little birds flew up into the air in a fright.

"That is because I am so ugly," thought the poor duckling, shutting his eyes, but he ran on all the same. Then he came to a great marsh where the wild ducks lived. He was so tired and miserable that he stayed there the whole night. In the morning the wild ducks flew up to inspect their new comrade.

"What sort of a creature are you?" they inquired, as the duckling turned from side to side and greeted them as well as he could. "You are frightfully ugly," said the wild ducks, "but that does not matter to us, so long as you do not marry into our family."

Poor fellow! He had not thought of marriage. All he wanted was permission to lie among the rushes and drink a little of the marsh water.

He stayed there two whole days. Then two wild geese came, or rather two wild ganders. They were not long out of the shell and therefore rather pert.

"I say, comrade," they said, "you are so ugly that we have taken quite a fancy to you! Will you join us and be a bird of passage? There is another marsh close by, and there are some charming wild geese there. All are sweet young ladies who can say quack! You are ugly enough to make your fortune among them." Just at that moment, "bang! bang!" was heard up above, and both the wild geese fell dead among the reeds, and the water turned blood red. "Bang! bang!" went the guns, and whole flocks of wild geese flew up from the rushes and the shots peppered among them again.

There was a grand shooting party, and the sportsmen lay hidden round the marsh. Some even sat on the branches of the trees which overhung the water. The blue smoke rose like clouds among the dark trees and swept over the pool.

The retrieving dogs wandered about in the swamp—splash! splash! The rushes and reeds bent beneath their tread on all sides. It was terribly alarming to the poor duckling. He twisted his head round to get it under his wing, and just at that moment a frightful big dog appeared close beside him. His tongue hung right out of his mouth, and his eyes glared wickedly. He opened his great chasm of a mouth close to the duckling, showed his sharp teeth, and—splash!—went on without touching him.

"Oh, thank Heaven!" sighed the duckling. "I am so ugly that even the dog won't bite me!"

Then he lay quite still while the shots whistled among the bushes, and bang after bang rent the air. Late in the day the noise ceased, but even then the poor duckling did not dare to get up. He waited several hours more before he looked about, and then he hurried away from the marsh as fast as he could. He ran across fields and meadow, and there was such a wind that he had hard work to make his way.

Towards night he reached a poor little cottage. It was such a miserable hovel that it remained standing only because it could not make up its mind which way to fall. The wind whistled so fiercely round the duckling that he had to sit on his tail to resist it, and it blew harder and ever harder. Then he saw that the door had fallen off one hinge and hung so crookedly that he could creep into the house through the crack, and by this means he made his way into the room.

An old woman lived here with her cat and her hen. The cat, whom she called, "Sonnie," could arch his back, purr, and even give off sparks, though for that you had to stroke his fur the wrong way. The hen had quite tiny short legs, and so she was called "Chickie-low-legs." She laid good eggs, and the old woman was as fond of her as if she had been her own child.

In the morning the strange duckling was discovered immediately, and the cat began to purr and the hen to cluck.

"What on earth is that?" said the old woman, looking round, but her sight was not good and she thought the duckling was a fat duck which had escaped. "This is a wonderful find!" said she. "Now I shall have duck's eggs—if only it is not a drake. We must wait and see about that."

So she took the duckling on trial for three weeks, but no eggs made their appearance. The cat was master of this house and the hen its mistress. They always said, "We and the world," for they thought that they represented the half of the world, and that quite the better half.

The duckling thought there might be two opinions on the subject, but the hen would not hear of it.

"Can you lay eggs?" she asked.

"No."

"Have the goodness to hold your tongue then!"

And the cat said, "Can you arch your back, purr, or give off sparks?"

"No."

"Then you had better keep your opinions to yourself when

people of sense are speaking!"

The duckling sat in the corner nursing his ill humor. Then he began to think of the fresh air and the sunshine, and an uncontrollable longing seized him to float on the water. At last he could not help telling the hen about it.

"What on earth possesses you?" she asked. "You have nothing to do. That is why you get these freaks into your head. Lay some eggs or take to purring, and you will get over it."

"But it is so delicious to float on the water," said the duckling. "It is so delicious to feel it rushing over your head when you dive to the bottom."

"That would be a fine amusement!" said the hen. "I think you have gone mad. Ask the cat about it. He is the wisest creature I know. Ask him if he is fond of floating on the water or diving under it. I say nothing about myself. Ask our mistress herself, the old woman. There is no one in the world cleverer than she is. Do you suppose she has any desire to float on the water or to duck underneath it?"

"You do not understand me," said the duckling.

"Well, if we don't understand you, who should? I suppose you don't consider yourself cleverer than the cat or the old woman, not to mention me! Don't make a fool of yourself, child, and thank your stars for all the good we have done you. Have you not lived in this warm room, and in such society that you might have learned something? But you are an idiot, and there is no pleasure in associating with you. You may believe me; I mean you well. I tell you home truths, and there is no surer way than that of knowing who are one's friends. You just set about laying some eggs, or learn to purr, or to emit sparks."

"I think I will go out into the wide world," said the duckling.

"Oh, do so by all means," said the hen.

So away went the duckling. He floated on the water and ducked underneath it, but he was looked askance at and slighted by every living creature for his ugliness. Now the autumn came on. The leaves in the woods turned yellow and brown. The wind took hold of them, and they danced about. The sky looked very cold and the clouds hung heavy with snow and hail. A raven stood on the fence and croaked, "Caw, caw!" from sheer cold. It made one shiver only to think of it. The poor duckling certainly was in a bad case!

One evening, the sun was just setting in wintry splendor when a flock of beautiful large birds appeared out of the bushes. The duckling had never seen anything so beautiful. They were dazzlingly white with long waving necks. They were swans, and uttering a peculiar cry they spread out their magnificent broad wings and flew away from the cold regions to warmer lands and open seas. They mounted so high, so very high, and the ugly little duckling became strangely uneasy. He circled round and round in the water like a wheel, craning his neck up into the air after them. Then he uttered a shriek so piercing and so strange that he was quite frightened by it himself.

Oh, he could not forget those beautiful birds, those happy birds. And as soon as they were out of sight he ducked right down to the bottom, and when he came up again he was quite beside himself. He did not know what the birds were, or whither they flew, but all the same he was more drawn towards them than he had ever been by any creatures before. He did not envy them in the least. How could it occur to him even to wish to be such a marvel of beauty? He would have been thankful if only the ducks would have tolerated him among them—the poor ugly creature.

The winter was so bitterly cold that the duckling was obliged

to swim about in the water to keep it from freezing over, but every night the hole in which he swam got smaller and smaller. Then it froze so hard that the surface ice cracked, and the duckling had to use his legs all the time so that the ice should not freeze around him. At last he was so weary that he could move no more, and he was frozen fast into the ice.

Early in the morning a peasant came along and saw him. He went out onto the ice and hammered a hole in it with his heavy wooden shoe, and carried the duckling home to his wife. There he soon revived. The children wanted to play with him, but the duckling thought they were going to ill-use him. In his fright he rushed into the milk pan, and the milk spurted out all over the room. The woman shrieked and threw up her hands. Then he flew into the butter cask, and down into the meal tub and out again. Just imagine what he looked like by this time! The woman screamed and tried to hit him with the fire tongs. The children tumbled over one another in trying to catch him, and they screamed with laughter. By good luck the door stood open, and the duckling flew out among the bushes and the newly fallen snow. And he lay there thoroughly exhausted.

But it would be too sad to mention all the privation and misery he had to go through during the hard winter. When the sun began to shine warmly again, the duckling was in the marsh, lying among the rushes. The larks were singing and the beautiful spring had come.

Then all at once he raised his wings and they flapped with much greater strength than before and bore him off vigorously. Before he knew where he was, he found himself in a large garden where the apple trees were in full blossom and the air was scented with lilacs, long branches of which overhung the shores of the lake. Oh, the spring freshness was delicious!

Just in front of him he saw three beautiful white swans advancing towards him from a thicket. With rustling feathers they swam lightly over the water. The duckling recognized the majestic birds, and he was overcome by a strange melancholy.

"I will fly to them, the royal birds, and they will hack me to pieces because I, who am so ugly, venture to approach them. But it won't matter! Better be killed by them than be snapped at by the ducks, pecked by the hens, spurned by the hen wife, or suffer so much misery in the winter."

So he flew into the water and swam towards the stately swans. They saw him and darted towards him with ruffled feathers.

"Kill me!" said the poor creature, and he bowed his head towards the water and awaited his death. But what did he see reflected in the transparent water?

He saw below him his own image, but he was no longer a clumsy dark gray bird, ugly and ungainly. He was himself a swan!

He felt quite glad of all the misery and tribulation he had gone through, for he was the better able to appreciate his good fortune now and all the beauty which greeted him. The big swans swam round and round him and stroked him with their bills.

Some little children came into the garden with corn and pieces of bread which they threw into the water, and the smallest one cried out, "There is a new one!" The other children shouted with joy, "Yes, a new one has come." And they clapped their hands and danced about, running after their father and mother. They threw the bread into the water, and one and all said, "The new one is the prettiest of them all. He is so young and handsome." And the old swans bent their heads and did homage before him.

He felt quite shy, and hid his head under his wing. He did not know what to think. He was very happy, but not at all proud, for a good heart never becomes proud. He thought of how he had been pursued and scorned, and now he heard them all say that he was the most beautiful of all beautiful birds. He raised his slender neck aloft, saying with exultation in his heart, "I never dreamt of so much happiness when I was the Ugly Duckling!"

How the Camel Got His Hump

by Rudyard Kipling

Now this is the next tale, and it tells how the Camel got his big hump.

In the beginning of years, when the world was so new and all, and the Animals were just beginning to work for Man, there was a Camel, and he lived in the middle of a Howling Desert because he did not want to work; and besides, he was a Howler himself. So he ate sticks and thorns and tamarisks and milkweed and prickles, most 'scruciating idle; and when anybody spoke to him he said "Humph!" Just "Humph!" and no more.

Presently the Horse came to him on Monday morning, with a saddle on his back and a bit in his mouth, and said,

"Camel, O Camel, come out and trot like the rest of us."

"Humph!" said the Camel; and the Horse went away and told the Man.

Presently the Dog came to him, with a stick in his mouth, and said, "Camel, O Camel, come and fetch and carry like the rest of us."

"Humph!" said the Camel; and the Dog went away and told the Man.

Presently the Ox came to him, with the yoke on his neck and said, "Camel, O Camel, come and plow like the rest of us."

"Humph!" said the Camel; and the Ox went away and told the Man.

At the end of the day the Man called the Horse and the Dog and the Ox together, and said, "Three, O Three, I'm very sorry for you (with the world so new-and-all); but that Humph-thing in the Desert can't work, or he would have been here by now, so I am going to leave him alone, and you must work double time to make up for it."

That made the Three very angry (with the world so new-and-

all), and they held a palaver, and an *indaba,* and a *punchayet,* and a pow-wow on the edge of the Desert; and the Camel came chewing milkweed *most* 'scruciating idle, and laughed at them. Then he said "Humph!" and went away again.

Presently there came along the Djinn in charge of All Deserts, rolling in a cloud of dust (Djinns always travel that way because it is Magic), and he stopped to palaver and pow-wow with the Three.

"Djinn of All Deserts," said the Horse, "*is* it right for any one to be idle, with the world so new-and-all?"

"Certainly not," said the Djinn.

"Well," said the Horse, "there's a thing in the middle of your Howling Desert (and he's a Howler himself) with a long neck and long legs, and he hasn't done a stroke of work since Monday morning. He won't trot."

"Whew!" said the Djinn, whistling, "that's my Camel, for all the gold in Arabia! What does he say about it?"

"He says, 'Humph!'" said the Dog; "and he won't fetch and carry."

"Does he say anything else?"

"Only 'Humph!'; and he won't plow," said the Ox.

"Very good," said the Djinn. "I'll humph him if you will kindly wait a minute."

The Djinn rolled himself up in his dust-cloak, and took a bearing across the desert, and found the Camel most 'scruciatingly idle, looking at his own reflection in a pool of water.

"My long and bubbling friend," said the Djinn, "what's this I hear of your doing no work, with the world so new-and-all?"

"Humph!" said the Camel.

The Djinn sat down, with his chin in his hand, and began to

think a Great Magic, while the Camel looked at his own reflection in the pool of water.

"You've given the Three extra work ever since Monday morning, all on account of your 'scruciating idleness," said the Djinn; and he went on thinking Magics, with his chin in his hand.

"Humph!" said the Camel.

"I shouldn't say that again if I were you," said the Djinn; "you might say it once too often. Bubbles, I want you to work."

And the Camel said, "Humph!" again; but no sooner had he said it than he saw his back, that he was so proud of, puffing up and puffing up into a great big lolloping humph.

"Do you see that?" said the Djinn. "That's your very own humph that you've brought upon your very own self by not working. To-day is Thursday, and you've done no work since Monday, when the work began. Now you are going to work."

"How can I," said the Camel, "with this humph on my back?"

"That's made a-purpose," said the Djinn, "all because you missed those three days. You will be able to work now for three days without eating, because you can live on your humph; and don't you ever say I never did anything for you. Come out of the Desert and go to the Three, and behave. Humph yourself!"

And the Camel humphed himself, humph and all, and went away to join the Three. And from that day to this the Camel always wears a humph (we call it "hump" now, not to hurt his feelings); but he has never yet caught up with the three days he missed at the beginning of the world, and he has never yet learned how to behave.

(From *Just So Stories*)

The WOLF
and the
SEVEN LITTLE KIDS

By Jakob and Wilhelm Grimm

Once upon a time there was an old goat who had seven little kids and loved them with all the love of a mother for her children. One day she wanted to go into the forest to get some food.

So she called all seven kids to her and said, "Dear children, I have to go into the forest. Be on your guard against the wolf. If he comes in, he will eat you up—skin, hair, and all. The wolf often disguises himself, but you will know him at once by his rough voice and his black feet."

The kids said, "Dear mother, we will take good care of ourselves. You may go away without any fear." Then the old goat bleated and went on her way with an easy mind.

It was not long before someone knocked at the house door and cried, "Open the door, dear children. Your mother is here and has brought something back with her for each of you."

But the little kids knew that it was the wolf because of the rough voice. "We will not open the door," they cried. "You are not our mother. She has a soft, pleasant voice, but your voice is rough. You are the wolf!"

Then the wolf went away to a shopkeeper and bought himself a big lump of chalk, ate this and made his voice soft with it. Then he came back, knocked at the door of the house, and cried, "Open the door, dear children. Your mother is here and has brought something back with her for each of you."

But the wolf had laid his black paws against the window, and the children saw them and cried, "We will not open the door. Our mother does not have black feet like yours. You are the wolf!"

Then the wolf ran to a baker and said, "I have hurt my feet. Rub some dough over them for me." And when the baker had rubbed his feet with dough, the wolf ran to the miller and said, "Sprinkle some white meal over my feet for me." The miller thought to himself, "The wolf wants to trick someone," and refused. But the wolf said, "If you will not do it, I will eat you up." Then the miller was afraid and made his paws white for him. Sometimes men are that way.

So now the wolf went for the third time to the house door, knocked at it and said, "Open the door for me, children. Your dear little mother has come home and has brought each of you something from the forest." The little kids cried, "First show us your paws so that we may know if you are our dear little mother." Then he put his paws in through the window. When the kids saw that they were white, they believed that all he had said was true and opened the door.

But who should come in but the wolf! They were terrified and wanted to hide themselves. One sprang under the table, the second into the bed, the third into the stove, the fourth into the kitchen, the fifth into the cupboard, the sixth under the washing-bowl, and the seventh into the clockcase.

But the wolf found them all and wasted no time. One right after another he swallowed them down his throat. The youngest in the clockcase was the only one that he did not find.

When the wolf was full, he left the house, lay down under a tree in the green meadow outside, and began to sleep.

Soon the old mother goat came home again from the forest. What a sight she saw there! The house door stood wide open. The table, chairs, and benches were thrown down. The washing-bowl lay broken to pieces. The quilts and pillows were pulled off the bed. She looked for her children, but they were nowhere to be found. She called them by name one by one, but no one answered. At last when she came to name the youngest, a soft voice cried, "Dear mother, I am in the clockcase."

She took the kid out, and it told her that the wolf had come and had eaten all the others. You can imagine how she wept over her poor children.

In her sorrow she went out after a while, and the youngest kid ran with her. When they came to the meadow, there lay the wolf by the tree, snoring so loudly that the branches shook. She looked at him closely and saw that something was moving and struggling in his overfed body.

"Ah, heavens," she said, "is it possible that my poor children, whom he has swallowed down for his supper, can be still alive?" She sent the kid running home to get scissors and a needle and thread. Then the mother goat cut open the wolf's stomach.

Hardly had she made one cut, then one little kid pushed its head out. And when she had cut farther, all six sprang out one after another. They were all still alive and had suffered no injury at all, because in his greediness the wolf had swallowed them down whole!

What rejoicing there was! They all hugged their dear mother and jumped like a tailor at his wedding.

But the mother said, "Now go and look for some big stones, and we will fill the evil beast's stomach with them while he is still asleep."

The seven kids quickly found some stones and put as many of them into his stomach as they could get in. The mother sewed him up again in the greatest haste, so that he was not aware of anything and never once moved.

When the wolf at last awoke, he got up. The stones in his stomach were making him very thirsty, he wanted to go to a well to drink. But when he began to walk and to move about, the stones in his stomach knocked against each other and rattled. Then he cried,

"What rumbles and tumbles
Against my poor bones?
I thought 'twas six kids
But it's only big stones."

And when he got to the well and stooped over the water ready to drink, the heavy stones made him fall in. There was no help, and he drowned miserably.

When the seven kids saw that, they came running to the spot and cried loudly, "The wolf is dead! The wolf is dead!" Then they danced for joy around the well with their mother.

(Adapted from
Grimm's Fairy Tales)

71

The Three Billy Goats Gruff

Retold by Gudrun Thorne-Thomsen

Once on a time there were three Billy Goats, who were to go up to the hillside to make themselves fat, and the family name of the goats was "Gruff."

On the way up was a bridge, over a river which they had to cross, and under the bridge lived a great ugly Troll with eyes as big as saucers and a nose as long as a poker.

First of all came the youngest Billy Goat Gruff to cross the bridge. "Trip, trap; trip, trap!" went the bridge.

"WHO'S THAT TRIPPING OVER MY BRIDGE?" roared the Troll.

"Oh, it is only I, the tiniest Billy Goat Gruff, and I'm going up to the hillside to make myself fat," said the Billy Goat, with such a small voice.

"Now, I'm coming to gobble you up," said the Troll.

"Oh, no, pray do not take me. I'm too little, that I am," said the Billy Goat. "Wait a bit till the second Billy Goat Gruff comes, he's much bigger."

"Well, be off with you," said the Troll.

A little while after came the second Billy Goat Gruff across the bridge.

"Trip, trap! Trip, trap!" went the bridge.

"WHO'S THAT TRIPPING OVER MY BRIDGE?" roared the Troll.

"Oh, it's the second Billy Goat Gruff, and I'm going up to the hillside to make myself fat," said the Billy Goat. Nor had he such a small voice either.

"Now, I'm coming to gobble you up!" said the Troll.

"Oh, no, don't take me. Wait a little till the big Billy Goat comes, he's much bigger."

"Very well! Be off with you," said the Troll.

But just then up came the big Billy Goat Gruff.

"Trip, trap! Trip, trap! Trip, trap!" went the bridge, for the Billy Goat was so heavy that the bridge creaked and groaned under him.

"WHO'S THAT TRAMPING ON MY BRIDGE?" roared the Troll.

"It is I! The big Billy Goat Gruff," said the Billy Goat, and he had a big hoarse voice.

"NOW, I'M COMING TO GOBBLE YOU UP!" roared the Troll.

> "Well come! I have two spears so stout,
> With them I'll thrust your eyeballs out;
> I have besides two great big stones,
> With them I'll crush you body and bones!"

That was what the big Billy Goat said; so he flew at the Troll, and thrust him with his horns, and tossed him out into the river, and after that he went up to the hillside.

There the Billy Goats got so fat that they were scarcely able to walk home again. And if they haven't grown thinner, why they're still fat; and so,

> "Snip, snap, stout.
> This tale's told out."

(From East o' the Sun and West o' the Moon)

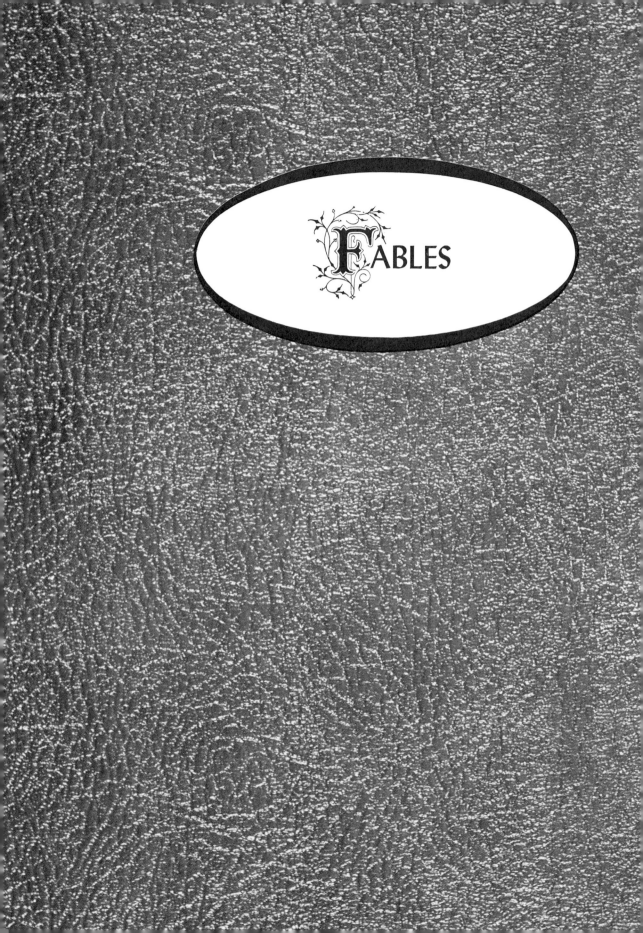

FABLES

THE SHEPHERD BOY AND THE WOLF

A young shepherd boy watched over his sheep every day while they ate grass. He passed the time by seeing how far he could throw a rock, or by looking at the clouds to see how many animal shapes he could find.

He liked his job well enough, but he longed for a little excitement. So, one day he decided to play a trick on the people of the village.

"Wolf! Wolf! Help!" he shouted as loud as he could.

Hearing the shepherd boy's cry, the people in the village picked up pitchforks and clubs and ran to help the boy save his sheep. When they arrived, they saw no wolf. They saw only the shepherd boy, doubled up with laughter.

"I fooled you. I fooled you," he giggled.

The people thought this was a very bad joke, indeed. They warned him not to call again, unless he was certain he saw a wolf.

The next week, the boy again played his trick on the villagers.

"Wolf! Wolf!" he cried out.

Once again, the people ran to his aid, and once again, they found no wolf—only the boy, laughing at them.

The next day, a wolf really did come down from the hills to help itself to a few fat sheep. "Wolf! Wolf!" yelled the shepherd boy with all the power in his lungs.

The people of the village heard his shouts for help and smiled. "He's trying to trick us again," they said, "but this time we won't be fooled."

Finally, the boy stopped shouting. He knew the villagers didn't believe him. He knew they wouldn't come. All he could do was stand back and watch the wolf kill his sheep.

People who tell lies find it hard to be believed, even when they tell the truth.

By Aesop

THE DOVE AND THE ANT

An Ant was speeding along on its three pair of legs when suddenly, it stopped.

"I'm thirsty," the Ant said aloud.

"Why don't you get a drink of water from the brook?" cooed a Dove perched in a nearby tree. "The brook is close by. Just be careful you don't fall in."

The Ant sped to the brook and began to drink.

A sudden wind blew the Ant into the water.

"Help!" the Ant cried, "I'm drowning!"

The Dove knew it had to act quickly to save the Ant. With its beak, the Dove broke a twig from the tree. Then, the Dove flew over the brook with the twig and dropped it to the Ant.

The Ant climbed onto the twig and floated ashore.

Not long afterward, the Ant saw a Hunter. He was setting a trap to catch the Dove.

The Dove began to fly toward the trap.

The Ant knew it had to act quickly to save the Dove.

The Ant opened its strong jaws and bit the bare ankle of the Hunter.

"Ouch!" the Hunter cried.

The Dove heard the Hunter and flew away.

One good turn deserves another.

By Aesop

THE HARE AND THE TORTOISE

By Aesop

The Hare was once boasting of his speed before the other animals. "I have never yet been beaten," said he, "when I put forth my full speed. I challenge anyone here to race with me."

The Tortoise said quietly, "I accept your challenge."

"That is a good joke," said the Hare. "I could dance round you all the way."

"Keep your boasting till you've beaten," answered the Tortoise. "Shall we race?"

So a course was fixed and a start was made. The Hare darted almost out of sight at once, but soon stopped and, to show his contempt for the Tortoise, lay down to have a nap.

The Tortoise plodded on and plodded on, and when the Hare awoke from his nap, he saw the Tortoise nearing the winning post, and could not run up in time to save the race. Then said the Tortoise,

"Slow but sure wins the race."

THE LION AND THE MOUSE

Once when a Lion was asleep a little Mouse began running up and down upon him. This soon wakened the Lion, who placed his huge paw upon the little Mouse, and opened his big jaws to swallow him.

"Pardon, O King," cried the little Mouse, "let me go this time and I shall never forget it. Who knows but what I may be able to do you a good turn some of these days?"

The Lion was so tickled at the idea of the Mouse being able to help him, that he lifted up his paw and let him go.

Some time later the Lion was caught in a trap. The hunters, who desired to carry him alive to the King, tied him to a tree while they went in search of a wagon to carry him on. Just then the little Mouse happened to pass by and, seeing the sad plight in which the Lion was, went up to him and soon gnawed away the ropes that bound the King of Beasts.

"Was I not right?" said the little Mouse.

Little friends may prove great friends.

By Aesop

The Crow and the Pitcher

By Aesop

   A crow, half-dead with thirst,
came upon a pitcher which had once been full of water;
but when the Crow put his beak into the mouth of the pitcher
he found that only very little water was left in it,
and that he could not reach far enough down to get at it.
He tried and he tried, but at last had to give up in despair.
   Then a thought came to him,
and he took a pebble and dropped it into the pitcher.
Then he took another pebble and dropped it into the pitcher.
Then he took another pebble and dropped that into the pitcher.
Then he took another pebble and dropped that into the pitcher.
Then he took another pebble and dropped that into the pitcher.
Then he took another pebble and dropped that into the pitcher.
At last, at last, he saw the water mount up near him,
and after casting in a few more pebbles
he was able to quench his thirst and save his life.
   Little by little does the trick.

FAIRY TALES

Sleeping Beauty

By Jakob and Wilhelm Grimm

A long time ago there lived a King and Queen, who said every day, "If only we had a child!" But for a long time they had none.

One day, as the Queen was bathing, a frog crept out of the water on to the land and said to her, "Your wish shall be fulfilled. Before a year has passed you shall bring a daughter into the world."

The frog's words came true. The Queen had a little girl who was so beautiful that the King could not contain himself for joy. He prepared a great feast and invited all his relations and friends and neighbors. He invited the fairies, too, in order that they might be kind and good to the child. There were thirteen of them in the kingdom, but as the King had only twelve golden plates for them to eat from, one of the fairies had to be left out.

The feast was held with all splendor, and when it came to an end, each of the fairies presented the child with a magic gift. One fairy gave her virtue, another beauty, a third riches, and so on, with everything in the world that she could wish for.

When eleven of the fairies had said their say, the thirteenth suddenly appeared. She wanted to show her spite for not having been invited. Without greeting anyone, or even glancing at anyone, she called out in a loud voice,

"When she is fifteen years old, the Princess shall prick herself with a spindle and shall fall down dead."

Then without another word she turned and left the hall.

Everyone was terror-stricken, but the twelfth fairy, whose wish was still not spoken, stepped forward. She could not take away the curse, but could only soften it, so she said,

"Your daughter shall not die, but shall fall into a deep sleep lasting a hundred years."

The King was so anxious to guard his dear child from this misfortune that he sent out a command that all the spindles in the whole kingdom should be burned.

All the promises of the fairies came true. The Princess grew up so beautiful, modest, kind, and clever that everybody who saw her could not but love her.

Now it happened that on the very day when she was fifteen years old the King and Queen were away from home, and the Princess was left quite alone in the castle. She wandered about over the whole place, looking at rooms and halls as she pleased, and at last she came to an old tower. She went up a narrow, winding staircase and reached a little door. A rusty key was sticking in the lock, and when she turned it the door flew open.

In a little room sat an old woman with a spindle, busily spinning her flax. This old woman was so deaf that she had never heard the King's command that all spindles should be destroyed.

"Good day, Granny," said the Princess, "what are you doing?"

"I am spinning," said the old woman, and nodded her head.

"What is the thing that whirls round so merrily?" asked the Princess, and she took the spindle and tried to spin, too.

But she had scarcely touched the spindle when it pricked her finger. At that moment she fell upon the bed which was standing near, and lay still in a deep sleep.

The King and Queen, who had just come home and had stepped into the hall, fell asleep, too, and all their courtiers with them. The horses fell asleep in the stable, the dogs in the yard, the doves on the roof, the flies on the wall. Yes, even the fire on the hearth grew still and went to sleep, and the meat that was roasting stopped crackling. The kitchen maid, who sat with a fowl before her, ready to pluck its feathers, fell asleep. The cook, too, who was pulling the kitchen boy's hair because he had made a mistake, let him go and both fell asleep. The wind dropped, and on the trees in front of the castle not a leaf stirred.

Round the castle a hedge of brier roses began to grow up. Every year it grew higher, till at last nothing could be seen of the castle.

There was a legend in the land about the lovely Sleeping Beauty, as the King's daughter was called, and from time to time Princes came and tried to force a way through the hedge into the castle. But they found it impossible, for the thorns, as though they had hands, held them fast, and the Princes remained caught in them without being able to free themselves, and so died.

After many, many years a Prince came again to the country and heard an old man tell of the castle which stood behind the brier hedge, in which a most beautiful maiden called Sleeping Beauty had been asleep for the last hundred years, and with her slept the King and Queen, and all their courtiers. He knew, also, from his grandfather, that many Princes had already come and sought to pierce through the brier hedge, and had been caught in it and died.

Then the young Prince said, "I am not afraid. I must go and see this Sleeping Beauty."

The good old man did all in his power to persuade him not to go, but the Prince would not listen to his words.

Now the hundred years were just ended. When the Prince approached the brier hedge it was covered with beautiful large blossoms. The shrubs made way for him of their own accord and let him pass unharmed, and then closed up again into a hedge.

In the courtyard he saw the horses and dogs lying asleep. On the roof sat the doves with their heads under their wings. When he went into the house the flies were asleep on the walls. Near the throne lay the King and Queen. In the kitchen the cook still had his hand raised as though to strike the kitchen boy, and the maid sat with the black fowl before her ready to pluck its feathers.

He went on farther. All was so still that he could hear his own breathing. At last he reached the tower, and opened the door into the little room where the Princess was asleep. There she lay, looking so beautiful that he could not take his eyes off her. He bent down and gave her a kiss. As he touched her, Sleeping Beauty opened her eyes and smiled at him.

Then they went down together. The King and the Queen and all the courtiers woke up, and looked at each other with astonished eyes. The horses in the stable stood up and shook them-

selves. The hounds leaped about and wagged their tails. The doves on the roof lifted their heads from under their wings, looked around, and flew into the fields. The flies on the walls began to crawl again. The fire in the kitchen roused itself and blazed up and cooked the food. The meat began to crackle, and the cook woke up and boxed the kitchen boy's ears so that he screamed aloud, while the maid finished plucking the fowl.

Then the Prince and Sleeping Beauty were married with all splendor, and they lived happily all their lives.

The Shoemaker and the Elves

By Jakob and Wilhelm Grimm

There was once a shoemaker, who, through no fault of his own, became so poor that at last he had nothing left but just enough leather to make one pair of shoes. He cut out the shoes at night, so as to set to work on them the next morning; and, as he had a good conscience, he laid himself quietly down in his bed, committed himself to heaven, and fell asleep. In the morning, after he had said his prayers, and was going to get to work, he found the pair of shoes made and finished, and standing on his table. He was very much astonished, and did not know what to think.

After a moment, the poor man took the shoes in his hand to examine them more carefully, and found them so well made that every stitch was in its right place, just as if they had come from the hand of a master workman.

Soon after, a purchaser entered, and as the shoes fitted him very well, he gave more than the usual price for them, so that the shoemaker had enough money to buy leather for two more pairs of shoes. He cut out the shoes at night, and intended to set to work the next morning with fresh spirit. But that was not to be, for when he got up, the two pairs of shoes were already finished, and even a customer was not lacking, who gave him so much money that he was able to buy leather enough for four new pairs. Early next morning he found the four pairs also finished, and so it always happened. Whatever he cut out in the evening was worked up by the morning, so that he was soon in the way of making a good living, and in the end became very well-to-do.

One night, not long before Christmas, when the shoemaker had finished cutting out, and before he went to bed, he said to his wife,

"How would it be if we were to sit up tonight and see who it is that does us this service?"

His wife agreed and set a light to burn. They both hid in a corner of the room, behind some coats that were hanging up, and then they began to watch. As soon as it was midnight, they saw come in two neatly formed naked little men, who seated themselves before the shoemaker's table, and took up the work that was already prepared. They began to stitch, to pierce, and to hammer so cleverly and quickly with their little fingers that the shoemaker's eyes could scarcely follow them, so full of wonder was he. And they never·left off until everything was finished and ready on the table, and then they jumped up and ran off.

The next morning the shoemaker's wife said to her husband, "Those little men have made us rich, and we ought to show ourselves grateful. With all their running about, and having nothing to cover them, they must be very cold. I'll tell you what: I will make little shirts, coats, waistcoats, and breeches for them, and knit each of them a pair of stockings, and you shall make each of them a pair of shoes."

The husband consented willingly, and at night, when everything was finished, they laid the gifts together on the table, instead of the cut-out work, and placed themselves so that they could observe how the little men would behave. When midnight came, they rushed in, ready to set to work, but when they found, instead of pieces of prepared leather, the neat little garments, they stood a moment in surprise, and then they showed the greatest delight. Swiftly they took up the pretty garments and slipped them on, singing,

What spruce and dandy boys are we!
No longer cobblers we will be.

Then they hopped and danced about, and at last they danced out at the door.

They were never seen again, but it went well with the shoemaker as long as he lived.　　　　　(Adapted from *Grimm's Fairy Tales*)

Lazy Jack

Adapted from an English fairy tale

Once upon a time there was a boy named Jack. He lived with his mother in a small house in a small village. Jack and his mother were very poor. What little they had the old woman earned by spinning wool into thread.

But Jack did nothing, for he was very lazy. In summer, he sat all day in the shade of a huge tree. In winter, he sat all day by the fire. His mother could not get him to do anything to help her. Finally, the old woman had had enough.

"You lazy boy!" she shouted, "if you do not go to work for your porridge I will turn you out of the house."

Frightened by his mother's threat, Jack thought he had best go to work if he wanted to eat. The very next day he went out and hired himself to a neighboring farmer for a penny. After he got his penny, Jack was very pleased. He had never had any money before. As he walked home, he kept tossing the penny into the air and catching it. But as he crossed a bridge, Jack dropped his penny. He watched in dismay as it rolled off the bridge and into the river below.

When his mother learned what had happened she was very angry. "You stupid boy," she said, "you should have put the penny in your pocket."

"I'll do so the next time," said Jack.

The next day Jack went out and hired himself to a cowherd. This man gave Jack a jar of milk for his day's work. Remember-

ing what his mother had said, Jack put the jar of milk into the large pocket of his jacket. Long before he got home, all the milk had spilled out.

"Dear me, you foolish boy," his mother said, "you should have carried the jar of milk on your head."

"I'll do so the next time," replied Jack.

The next day Jack again hired himself to a farmer. The farmer agreed to give Jack a cream cheese for his work. In the evening, Jack took the cheese. Remembering what his mother had said, Jack put the cheese on his head, and started home. But by the time he got home most of the cheese had melted and run into his hair.

"You stupid lout," his mother shouted, "you should have carried the cheese very carefully in your hands."

"I'll do so the next time," replied Jack.

The following day Jack went out and hired himself to a baker. When Jack had finished work, the baker give him a large tomcat. Remembering what his mother had said, Jack carried the cat very carefully in his hands. But in a short time the cat had scratched him so much he had to let it go.

When he got home, his mother said to him, "You silly boy. You should have tied a string to the cat and dragged it along after you."

"I'll do so the next time," replied Jack.

The next day Jack hired himself to a butcher. This good man paid Jack with a leg of lamb. Remembering what his mother had said, Jack tied a string to the leg of lamb and dragged it through the dirt after him. By the time Jack reached home, the meat was spoiled.

This time, Jack's mother was out of patience with him. The next day was Sunday, and now they would have nothing but boiled cabbage for their Sunday dinner.

"You ninny-hammer," she cried, "you should have carried the leg of lamb on your shoulder."

"I'll do so the next time," replied Jack.

Well, on Monday, Lazy Jack went out once more to look for work. This time he hired himself to a cattlekeeper. At the end of the day, the man gave Jack a donkey. Remembering what his mother had said, Jack hoisted the donkey onto his shoulders. Although he was very strong, Jack had difficulty doing this. At last, however, he got the donkey up on his shoulders and started home.

Now it happened that on his way home Jack had to pass the house of a very rich man. This man had an only daughter, who was very beautiful. Unfortunately, she could not speak or hear, and she had never laughed in her life. The doctors had told her father that she would never speak or hear until someone made her laugh. Many people tried, but without success. At last despairing of all hope, her father offered to give her in marriage to the first man who could make her laugh.

Now it happened that the young lady was looking out the window as Jack struggled along with the donkey on his shoulders. The poor beast, its legs sticking up in the air, was kicking violently and hee-hawing with all its might. Well, the sight was so funny the young lady burst into laughter. Instantly she recovered her speech and her hearing.

Her father was overjoyed. He kept his promise, and gave her to Jack in marriage. He also made Jack a rich man.

After Jack and the girl were married, they went to live in a large house. And Jack's mother lived with them in great happiness for the rest of her life.

RAPUNZEL

By Jakob and Wilhelm Grimm

Once upon a time there were a man and a woman who had long wished for a child in vain. In time the woman knew that she was about to have a child. These people could see a splendid garden from their house. It was full of the most beautiful flowers and herbs. But it belonged to a witch who had great power and was feared by all. No one dared go over the wall that surrounded the garden for fear of the witch.

One day the woman was standing by this window and looking down into the garden, when she saw a bed of the most beautiful flowering plant, called rapunzel. It looked so fresh and green that she longed for it. This longing increased every day.

Because she knew that she could not get any of it, she pined away and looked pale and miserable. Then her husband became alarmed and asked, "What ails you, dear wife?"

"Ah," she replied, "if I can't have some of the rapunzel, in the garden behind our house to eat, I shall die."

The man, who loved her, thought, "Sooner than let my wife die, I shall bring her some of the rapunzel, no matter what the danger."

In the twilight of evening, he climbed down over the wall into the garden of the witch, hastily clutched a handful of rapunzel, and took it to his wife. She at once made herself a salad of it and ate it with much delight.

She liked it so much that the next day she longed for it three times as much as before. If he was to have any rest, her husband must once more climb down into the garden.

So in the gloom of evening, he let himself down again. But when he had reached the bottom, he was terribly afraid for he saw the witch standing before him.

"How dare you," she said with an angry look, "to climb into my garden and steal my rapunzel like a thief? You shall suffer for it!"

"Ah," he answered, "let mercy take the place of justice. I made up my mind to do it only out of necessity. My wife saw your rapunzel from the window and felt such a longing for it that she would have died if she had not gotten some to eat."

Then the witch allowed her anger to be softened and said to him, "If the case be as you say, I will allow you to take away with you as much rapunzel as you wish, only I make one condition. You must give me the child that your wife will bring into the world. It shall be well treated, and I will care for it like a mother."

The man in his terror agreed to everything, and when the child was born the witch appeared at once, gave the child the name of Rapunzel, and took it away with her.

Rapunzel grew into the most beautiful child beneath the sun. When she was twelve years old, the witch shut her into a tower, which lay in a forest. The tower had neither stairs nor doors, but at the very top was a little window. When the witch wanted to go in, she stood beneath this and cried,

Rapunzel, Rapunzel,
Let down your hair to me.

Rapunzel had magnificent long hair, fine as spun gold. And when she heard the voice of the witch, she untied her braided tresses, wound them around one of the hooks of the window, and then the hair fell twenty lengths down, and the witch climbed up by it.

After a year or two, it happened that the King's son rode through the forest and went by the tower. Then he heard a song, which was so charming that he stood still and listened.

The song was from Rapunzel singing. In her loneliness, she passed her time in letting her sweet voice sound. The King's son wanted to climb up to her and looked for the door of the tower, but none was to be found.

He rode home, but the singing had so deeply touched his heart, that every day he went out into the forest and listened to it. Once when he was standing behind a tree, he saw that a witch came there, and he heard how she cried,

Rapunzel, Rapunzel,
Let down your hair.

Then Rapunzel would let down the braids of her hair, and the

witch would climb up to her.

"If that is the ladder by which one mounts, I will for once try my fortune," he said. And the next day when it began to grow dark, he went to the tower and cried,

> *Rapunzel, Rapunzel,*
> *Let down your hair.*

Immediately the hair fell down and the King's son climbed up.

At first Rapunzel was terribly frightened for she had never seen a man before. But the King's son began to talk to her quite like a friend and told her that his heart had been so stirred that it had let him have no rest, and he had been forced to see her. Then Rapunzel lost her fear.

And when he asked her if she would take him for her husband and she saw that he was young and handsome, she thought, "He will love me more than the old witch does." And so she said yes and laid her hand in his.

She said, "I will willingly go away with you, but I do not know how to get down. Bring with you a roll of silk every time that you come, and I will weave a ladder with it. When that is ready, I will climb down and you will take me away on your horse."

They agreed that until that time he should come to her every evening, for the old woman came by day.

The witch knew nothing of all this until once Rapunzel forgot and said to her, "Tell me, old witch, how it happens that you are so much heavier for me to draw up than the young King's son— he is with me in a moment."

"Ah! you wicked child," cried the witch. "What do I hear you say! I thought I had separated you from all the world, and yet you have tricked me!"

In her anger she clutched Rapunzel's beautiful tresses, wrapped them twice round her left hand, seized a pair of scissors with the right, and snip, snap, they were cut off and the lovely braids lay on the ground. And she was so pitiless that she took poor Rapunzel into a desert where she had to live in great grief and misery.

On the same day that she cast out Rapunzel the witch that evening tied onto the hook of the window the braids of hair which she had cut from Rapunzel's head. And when the King's son came and cried:

Rapunzel, Rapunzel,
Let down your hair.

she let the hair down.

The King's son climbed up, but he did not find his dearest Rapunzel above. Instead there was the witch who gazed at him with wicked and hateful looks.

"Aha!" she cried scornfully. "You would fetch your dearest, but the beautiful bird sits no longer singing in the nest. The cat has got it and will scratch out your eyes as well. Rapunzel is lost to you. You will never see her again."

The King's son was beside himself with pain, and in his despair he leapt down from the tower. He escaped with his life, but the thorns into which he fell pierced his eyes.

Then he wandered blind about the forest, ate nothing but roots and berries, and did nothing but lament and weep over the loss of his dearest. In this condition he wandered about in misery for some years. In time he happened to wander into the desert where Rapunzel lived in wretchedness.

He heard a voice, and it seemed so familiar to him that he went toward it. When he approached, Rapunzel recognized him and fell on his neck and wept. Two of her tears of love wetted his eyes. Suddenly his blind eyes grew clear again, and he could see with them as before.

He led her to his kingdom where he was joyfully welcomed, and they lived happily ever after. (Adapted from *Grimm's Fairy Tales*)

The Bremen Town Musicians

By Jakob and Wilhelm Grimm

A certain man had a donkey that had carried the corn sacks to the mill untiringly for many years. But his strength was going, and he was growing more and more unfit for work. Then his master began to think that the donkey wasn't worth his hay. But the donkey, seeing the harm that might come to him, ran away

and started out on the road to Bremen. "There," he thought, "I can surely be the town musician."

When he had walked some distance, he found a hound lying on the road, panting like one who had run till he was tired. "What are you panting so for, you big fellow?" asked the donkey.

"Ah," replied the hound, "as I am old and grow weaker every day and can hunt no more, my master wanted to kill me. So I ran away. But now how am I to earn a living?"

"I tell you what," said the donkey, "I am going to Bremen and shall be town musician there. Go with me and become a musician also."

The hound agreed, and on they went.

Before long they came to a cat, sitting on the path, with a face as sad as three rainy days! "Now then, old one, what has gone wrong with you?" asked the donkey.

"Who can be merry when his life is in danger?" answered the cat. "I am now getting old. My teeth are worn to stumps. I prefer to sit by the fire and sleep, rather than hunt about after mice. So my mistress wanted to drown me. That's why I ran away. But now what am I to do? Where am I to go?"

"Go with us to Bremen. You understand night music, so you can be a town musician."

The cat thought it was a good idea and went with them. After this the three of them came to a farmyard where the cock was sitting upon the gate, crowing with all his might. "Your crowing chills my bones," said the donkey. "What is the matter?"

"I have been predicting fine weather because it is the day on which the housewife washes her child's little shirts and wants to dry them," said the cock. "But guests are coming for Sunday, so the housewife has no pity and has told the cook that she intends to eat me in the soup tomorrow. And this evening I am to have my head cut off. Now I am crowing loudly while I can."

"Ah, cock," said the donkey, "you had better come away with us. We are going to Bremen. You can find something better than death there. You have a good voice, and if we make music together it must have some quality!"

The cock agreed to this plan, and all four went on together. But they could not reach the city of Bremen in one day. In the evening they came to a forest where they decided to spend the night. The donkey and the hound lay down under a large tree, while the cat and the cock settled themselves in the branches. But the cock flew right to the top where he would be the safest of all. Before he went to sleep, he looked all around and thought he saw in the distance a little spark of light burning. He called out to his companions that there must be a house not far off, for he saw a light. The donkey said, "If so, we had better get up and go on, for the shelter here is bad." The hound thought that a few bones with some meat on them would do him good, too!

So they made their way to the place where the light was and soon saw it shine brighter and grow larger until they came to a well-lighted robber's house. The donkey, as he was the biggest, went to the window and looked in.

"What do you see, my donkey?" asked the cock. "What do I see?" answered the donkey. "I see a table covered with good things to eat and drink, and robbers sitting at it enjoying themselves." "That would be the sort of thing for us," said the cock. "Yes, yes. Ah, how I wish we were there!" said the donkey.

Then the animals talked together of how they should drive away the robbers. At last they thought of a plan. The donkey was to place himself with his forefeet upon the window ledge, the hound was to jump on the donkey's back, the cat was to climb upon the dog, and lastly the cock was to fly up and perch upon the head of the cat.

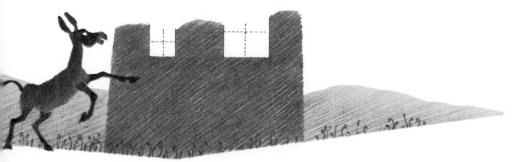

When this was done, at a certain signal, they began to perform their music together. The donkey brayed. The hound barked. The cat meowed. And the cock crowed. Then they burst through the window into the room so that the glass shattered! At this horrible noise the robbers sprang up, thinking that a ghost had come in, and fled in fear out into the forest. The four companions now sat down at the table, well pleased with what was left and ate as if they would not eat for a month.

As soon as the four musicians had finished, they put out the light, and each looked for a suitable sleeping place for himself. The donkey lay down upon some straw in the yard, the hound behind the door, the cat upon the hearth near the warm ashes, and the cock perched himself upon a beam of the roof. And, being tired with their long walk, they soon went to sleep.

When it was past midnight, and the robbers saw from afar that the light was no longer burning in their house and that all appeared quiet, the leader said, "We shouldn't have let ourselves be frightened so." And he ordered one of them to go and inspect the house.

The messenger finding all still went into the kitchen to light a candle and, taking the shining fiery eyes of the cat for live coals, he held a match to them to light it. But the cat did not understand the action and flew in his face, spitting and scratching. The robber was so frightened that he ran to the back door. But the dog, who lay there, sprang up and bit his leg. And as he ran across the yard by the straw-pile, the donkey gave him a hard kick with its hind foot. The cock, too, who had been awakened by the noise, and had become excited, cried down from the beam, "Cock-a-doodle-doo!"

Then the robber ran back as fast as he could to his leader and said, "Ah, there is a horrible witch sitting in the house, who spat on me and scratched my face with her long claws. And by the door stands a man with a knife who stabbed me in the leg. And in the yard there lies a black monster who beat me with a wooden club. And above, upon the roof, sits the judge who called out, 'Bring the villain here to me!' So I got away as well as I could."

After this the robbers did not trust themselves in the house again. But it suited the four musicians of Bremen so well that they did not care to leave it any more.

(Adapted from *Grimm's Fairy Tales*)

If you are ever in the city of Bremen, Germany, you can visit this monument which was built in honor of the Bremen town musicians.

GUDBRAND-ON-THE-HILLSIDE

Retold by Gudrun Thorne-Thomsen

Once upon a time there was a man whose name was Gud-brand. He had a farm which lay far, far away upon a hillside, and so they called him Gudbrand-on-the-Hillside.

Now, you must know this man and his good wife lived so happily together, and understood one another so well, that all

110

111

the husband did the wife thought so well done there was nothing like it in the world, and she was always pleased at whatever he turned his hand to. The farm was their own land, and they had a hundred dollars lying at the bottom of their chest and two cows tethered up in a stall in their farmyard.

So one day his wife said to Gudbrand, "Do you know, dear, I think we ought to take one of our cows into town and sell it; that's what I think; for then we shall have some money in hand, and such well-to-do people as we ought to have ready money as other folks have. As for the hundred dollars in the chest yonder, we can't make a hole in our savings, and I'm sure I don't know what we want with more than one cow.

"Besides, we shall gain a little in another way, for then I shall get off with only looking after one cow, instead of having, as now, to feed and litter and water two."

Well, Gudbrand thought his wife talked right good sense, so he set off at once with the cow on the way to town to sell her; but when he got to the town, there was no one who would buy his cow.

"Well, well, never mind," said Gudbrand, "at the worst, I can only go back home with my cow. I've both stable and tether for her, and the road is no farther out than in." And with that he began to toddle home with his cow.

But when he had gone a bit of the way, a man met him who had a horse to sell. Gudbrand thought 'twas better to have a horse than a cow, so he traded with the man. A little farther on he met a man walking along and driving a fat pig before him, and he thought it better to have a fat pig than a horse, so he traded with the man. After that he went a little farther, and a man met him with a goat, so he thought it better to have a goat than a pig, and he traded with the man who owned the goat.

Then he went on a good bit till he met a man who had a sheep, and he traded with him, too, for he thought it always better to have a sheep than a goat. After a while he met a man with a goose, and he traded away the sheep for the goose; and when he had walked a long, long time, he met a man with a cock, and he traded with him, for he thought in this way, " 'Tis surely better to have a cock than a goose."

Then he went on till the day was far spent, and he began to get very hungry, so he sold the cock for a shilling, and bought food with the money, for, thought Gudbrand-on-the-Hillside, " 'Tis always better to save one's life than to have a cock."

After that he went on homeward till he reached his nearest neighbor's house, where he turned in.

"Well," said the owner of the house, "how did things go with you in town?"

"Rather so-so," said Gudbrand, "I can't praise my luck, nor do I blame it either," and with that he told the whole story from first to last.

"Ah!" said his friend, "you'll get nicely hauled over the coals, when you go home to your wife. Heaven help you, I wouldn't stand in your shoes for anything."

"Well," said Gudbrand-on-the-Hillside, "I think things might have gone much worse with me; but now, whether I have done wrong or not, I have so kind a good wife she never has a word to say against anything that I do."

"Oh!" answered his neighbor, "I hear what you say, but I don't believe it for all that."

"And so you doubt it?" asked Gudbrand-on-the-Hillside.

"Yes," said the friend. "I have a hundred crowns, at the bottom of my chest at home, I will give you if you can prove what you say."

So Gudbrand stayed there till evening, when it began to get dark, and then they went together to his house, and the neighbor was to stand outside the door and listen, while the man went in to his wife.

"Good evening!" said Gudbrand-on-the-Hillside.

"Good evening!" said the good wife. "Oh! is that you? Now, I am happy."

Then the wife asked how things had gone with him in town.

"Oh, only so-so," answered Gudbrand; "not much to brag of. When I got to town there was no one who would buy the cow, so you must know I traded it away for a horse."

"For a horse," said his wife; "well that is good of you; thanks with all my heart. We are so well to do that we may drive to church just as well as other people, and if we choose to keep a horse we have a right to get one, I should think." So, turning to her child she said, "Run out, deary, and put up the horse."

"Ah!" said Gudbrand, "but you see I have not the horse after all, for when I got a bit farther on the road, I traded it for a pig."

"Think of that, now!" said the wife. "You did just as I should have done myself; a thousand thanks! Now I can have a bit of bacon in the house to set before people when they come to see me, that I can. What do we want with a horse? People would only say we had got so proud that we couldn't walk to church. Go out, child, and put up the pig in the sty."

"But I have not the pig either," said Gudbrand, "for when I got a little farther on, I traded it for a goat."

"Dear me!" cried the wife, "how well you manage everything! Now I think it over, what should I do with a pig? People would only point at us and say 'Yonder they eat up all they have.' No, now I have a goat, and I shall have milk and cheese, and keep the goat, too. Run out, child, and put up the goat."

"Nay, but I haven't the goat either," said Gudbrand, "for a little farther on I traded it away and got a fine sheep instead!"

"You don't say so!" cried his wife, "why, you do everything to please me, just as if I had been with you. What do we want with a goat? If I had it I should lose half my time in climbing up the hills to get it down. No, if I have a sheep, I shall have both wool and clothing, and fresh meat in the house. Run out, child, and put up the sheep."

"But I haven't the sheep any more than the rest," said Gudbrand, "for when I got a bit farther, I traded it away for a goose."

"Thank you, thank you, with all my heart," cried his wife, "what should I do with a sheep? I have no spinning wheel or carding comb, nor should I care to worry myself with cutting, and shaping, and sewing clothes. We can buy clothes now as we have always done; and now I shall have roast goose, which I have longed for so often; and, besides, down with which to stuff my little pillow. Run out, child, and put up the goose."

"Well!" said Gudbrand, "I haven't the goose either; for when I had gone a bit farther I traded it for a cock."

"Dear me!" cried his wife, "how you think of everything! Just as I should have done myself. A cock! Think of that! Why it's as good as an eight-day clock, for every day the cock crows at four o'clock, and we shall be able to stir our stiff legs in good time. What should we do with a goose? I don't know how to cook it; and as for my pillow, I can stuff it with cotton grass. Run out, child, and put up the cock."

"But after all, I haven't the cock either," said Gudbrand, "for when I had gone a bit farther, I became as hungry as a hunter, so I was forced to sell the cock for a shilling, for fear I should starve."

"Now, God be praised that you did so!" cried his wife, "whatever you do, you do it always just after my own heart. What should we do with the cock? We are our own masters, I should think, and can lie abed in the morning as long as we like. Heaven be thanked that I have you safe back again; you who do everything so well, that I want neither cock nor goose; neither pigs nor kine."

Then Gudbrand opened the door and said, "Well, what do you say now? Have I won the hundred crowns?" and his neighbor was forced to admit that he had.

(From *East o' the Sun and West o' the Moon*)

THE EMPEROR'S NEW CLOTHES

By Hans Christian Andersen

Many years ago there was an Emperor who was so excessively fond of new clothes that he spent all his money on them. He cared nothing about his soldiers or for the theater, or for driving in the woods, except for the sake of showing off his new clothes. He had a costume for every hour in the day. Instead of saying, as one does about any other King or Emperor, "He is in his council chamber," the people here always said, "The Emperor is in his dressing room."

Life was very gay in the great town where he lived. Hosts of strangers came to visit it, and among them one day were two swindlers. They gave themselves out as weavers and said that they knew how to weave the most beautiful fabrics imaginable. Not only were the colors and patterns unusually fine, but the clothes that were made of this cloth had the peculiar quality of becoming invisible to every person who was not fit for the office he held, or who was impossibly dull.

"Those must be splendid clothes," thought the Emperor. "By wearing them I should be able to discover which men in my kingdom are unfitted for their posts. I shall be able to tell the wise men from the fools. Yes, I certainly must order some of that stuff to be woven for me."

The Emperor paid the two swindlers a lot of money in advance, so that they might begin their work at once.

They did put up two looms and pretended to weave, but they had nothing whatever upon their shuttles. At the outset they asked for a quantity of the finest silk and the purest gold thread, all of which they put into their own bags while they worked away at the empty looms far into the night.

"I should like to know how those weavers are getting on with their cloth," thought the Emperor, but he felt a little queer when he reflected that anyone who was stupid or unfit for his post would not be able to see it. He certainly thought that he need have no fears for himself. Still he thought he would send somebody else first to see how the work was getting on. Everybody in the town knew what wonderful power the stuff possessed, and every one was anxious to see how stupid his neighbor was.

"I will send my faithful old minister to the weavers," thought the Emperor. "He will be best able to see how the stuff looks, for he is a clever man and no one fulfills his duties better than he does!"

So the good old minister went into the room where the two swindlers sat working at the empty loom.

"Heaven help us," thought the old minister, opening his eyes very wide. "Why, I can't see a thing!" But he took care not to say so.

Both the swindlers begged him to be good enough to step a little nearer. They asked if he did not think it a good pattern and beautiful coloring, and they pointed to the empty loom. The poor old minister stared as hard as he could, but he could not see anything, for of course there was nothing to see.

"Good heavens!" thought he. "Is it possible that I am a fool?

I have never thought so, and nobody must know it. Am I not fit for my post? It will never do to say that I cannot see the stuff."

"Well, sir, you don't say anything about the stuff," said the one who was pretending to weave.

"Oh, it is beautiful! Quite charming," said the minister, looking through his spectacles. "Such a pattern and such colors! I will certainly tell the Emperor that the stuff pleases me very much."

"We are delighted to hear you say so," said the swindlers, and then they named all the colors and described the peculiar pattern. The old minister paid close attention to what they said, so as to be able to repeat it when he got home to the Emperor.

Then the swindlers went on to demand more money, more silk, and more gold, to be able to proceed with the weaving. They put it all into their own pockets. Not a single strand was ever put into the loom. But they went on as before, pretending to weave at the empty loom.

The Emperor soon sent another faithful official to see how the stuff was getting on and if it would soon be ready. The same thing happened to him as to the minister. He looked and looked, but as there was only the empty loom, he could see nothing at all.

"Is not this a beautiful piece of stuff?" said both the swindlers, showing and explaining the beautiful pattern and colors which were not there to be seen.

"I know I am no fool," thought the man, "so it must be that I am unfit for my good post. It is very strange, but I must not let on." So he praised the stuff he did not see, and assured the swindlers of his delight in the beautiful colors and the originality of the design. "It is absolutely charming!" he said to the Emperor.

Everybody in the town was now talking about this splendid stuff, and the Emperor thought he would like to see it while it was still on the loom. So, accompanied by a number of selected courtiers, among whom were the two faithful officials who had already seen the imaginary stuff, he went to visit the crafty impostors. They were working away as hard as ever they could at the empty loom.

"It is magnificent!" said both the honest officials. "Only see, Your Majesty, what a design! What colors!" And they pointed to the empty loom, for they each thought the others could see the stuff.

"What!" thought the Emperor. "I see nothing at all. This is terrible! Am I a fool? Am I not fit to be Emperor? Why, nothing worse could happen to me!

"Oh, it is beautiful," said the Emperor. "It has my highest approval." He nodded his satisfaction as he gazed at the empty loom. Nothing would induce him to say that he could not see anything.

The whole suite gazed and gazed, but saw nothing more than all the others. However, they all exclaimed with His Majesty, "It is very beautiful!" They advised him to wear a suit made of this wonderful cloth on the occasion of a great procession which was just about to take place. "Magnificent! Gorgeous! Excellent!"

went from mouth to mouth. They were all equally delighted with it. The Emperor gave each of the weavers an order of knighthood to be worn in his buttonhole and the title of "Gentleman Weaver."

The swindlers sat up the whole night before the day on which the procession was to take place. They burned sixteen candles, so that people might see how anxious they were to get the Emperor's new clothes ready. They pretended to take the stuff off the loom. They cut it out in the air with a huge pair of scissors, and they stitched away with needles without any thread in them.

At last they said, "Now the Emperor's new clothes are ready."

The Emperor, with his grandest courtiers, went to them himself. Both the swindlers raised one arm in the air, as if they were holding something. They said, "See, these are the trousers. This is the coat. Here is the mantle," and so on. "They are as light as a spider's web. One might think one had nothing on, but that is the very beauty of it."

"Yes," said all the courtiers, but they could not see anything, for there was nothing to see.

"Will Your Imperial Majesty be graciously pleased to take off your clothes?" said the impostors. "Then we may put on the new ones, along here before the great mirror."

The Emperor took off all his clothes, and the impostors pretended to give him one article of dress after the other of the new clothes which they had pretended to make. They pretended to fasten something around his waist and to tie on something. This was the train. The Emperor turned round and round in front of the mirror.

"How well His Majesty looks in the new clothes! How becoming they are!" cried all the people. "What a design, and what colors! They are most gorgeous robes!"

"The canopy is waiting outside which is to be carried over Your Majesty in the procession," said the master of ceremonies.

"Well, I am quite ready," said the Emperor. "Don't the

clothes fit well?" Then he turned round again in front of the mirror, so that he should seem to be looking at his grand things.

The chamberlains who were to carry the train stooped and pretended to lift it from the ground with both hands, and they walked along with their hands in the air. They dared not let it appear that they could not see anything.

Then the Emperor walked along in the procession under the gorgeous canopy, and everybody in the streets and at the windows exclaimed, "How beautiful the Emperor's new clothes are! What a splendid train! And they fit to perfection!" Nobody would let it appear that he could see nothing, for that would prove that he was not fit for his post, or else he was a fool. None of the Emperor's clothes had been so successful before.

"But he has nothing on," said a little child.

"Oh, listen to the innocent," said its father. And one person whispered to the other what the child had said. "He has nothing on—a child says he has nothing on!"

"But he has nothing on!" at last cried all the people.

The Emperor writhed, for he knew it was true. But he thought, "The procession must go on now." So he held himself stiffer than ever, and the chamberlains held up the invisible train.

(From Andersen's Fairy Tales)

FAVORITES OLD AND NEW

LITTLE TOOT

By Hardie Gramatky

At the foot of an old, old wharf lives the cutest, silliest little tugboat you ever saw. A *very* handsome tugboat with a brand-new candy-stick smokestack.

His name is Little Toot. And this name he came by through no fault of his own. Blow hard as he would, the only sound that came out of his whistle was a gay, small -toot-toot-toot.

But what he couldn't create in sound, Little Toot made up for in smoke. From his chubby smokestack he would send up a volley of smoke balls which bubbled over his wake like balloons. Hence, when he got all "steamed up," Little Toot used to feel very important . . .

Then the flag at his masthead would dance like the tail of a puppy dog when he's happy . . .

And he flaunted his signals like a man-o'-war.

Now, the river where Little Toot lives is full of ships. They come from ports all over the world, bringing crews who speak strange tongues, and bringing even stranger cargoes—hides from Buenos Aires, copra from the South Seas, whale oil from the Antarctic, and fragrant teas from distant Asia. So there is always work for tugboats to do, either pushing ships into the docks to be unloaded, or else pulling them into the stream and down the channel to the ocean to begin a new voyage.

So a tugboat's life is a busy, exciting one, and Little Toot was properly right in the middle of it. His father, Big Toot, is the biggest and fastest tugboat on the river. Why, Big Toot can make *more* smoke and kick up *more* water than any two of the other boats put together.

As for Grandfather Toot, he is an old sea dog who breathes smoke . . . and tells of his mighty deeds on the river.

You'd think that Little Toot, belonging to such an important family, would have his mind on work. But no. Little Toot hated work. He saw no sense in pulling ships fifty times bigger than himself all the way down to the ocean. And he was scared of the wild seas that lay in wait outside the channel, beyond where the harbor empties into the ocean.

Little Toot had no desire to be tossed around. He preferred the calm water of the river itself, where he could always find plenty of fun. Like gliding, for example . . .

Or playing thread-the-needle around the piers.

Or, what was even fancier, cutting figure 8's . . .

Little Toot liked nothing better than to make a really fine figure 8. First you throw your weight on one side, then on the other. And the result never failed to delight him, although his antics annoyed the hard-working tugboats awfully.

But he kept on making figure 8's that grew bigger and bigger until one day, carried away by the joy of it all, he made one so big it took up the whole river. Indeed, there was hardly room for it between the two shores . . .

And no room at all for a big tug named J. G. McGillicuddy, which was bound downstream to pick up a string of coal barges from Hoboken. J. G. McGillicuddy had little love for other tugboats, anyway, and a frivolous one like Little Toot made him mad.

This by itself was bad enough; but, unfortunately for Little Toot, the other tugboats had seen what had happened. So they began to make fun of him, calling him a sissy who only knew how to play . . .

Poor Little Toot. He was ashamed and angry, but there was nothing he could do about it except blow those silly smoke balls . . .

But the more he blew, the more the other boats laughed at him.

Little Toot couldn't stand it. He fled to his favorite hiding place alongside the wharf, where his taunting friends could not reach him; and there he just sat and sulked.

After he had moped a while Little Toot saw, headed down the river, a great ocean liner.

And pulling it were four tugboats, with his own father Big Toot right up in front.

The sight of that brave, bustling work made Little Toot think. He thought harder than ever in his life, and then—all of a sudden —a great idea burst over him. He *wouldn't* be a silly, frivolous little tugboat any more. He would work like the best of them. After all, wasn't he the son of Big Toot, the mightiest tug on the river? Well, he would make Big Toot proud of him. He'd show them all! Full of ambition, he started eagerly downstream.

He sidled hopefully up to one big ship after another, tooting for them to heave a towline. But they supposed he was still only a nuisance, and would have nothing to do with him. Oscar, the Scandinavian, rudely blew steam in his face . . .

. . . And the others were too busy with their own affairs to notice a bothersome little tug. They knew him too well!

But the rudest of all was a great transatlantic liner which blasted him right out of the water.

That was too much for Little Toot. He wasn't wanted anywhere or by anyone. With his spirits drooping he let the tide carry him where it willed. He was so *lonesome* . . .

Floating aimlessly downstream he grew sadder and sadder until he was utterly miserable. He was sunk so deep in his own despair he didn't even notice that the sky had grown dark and that the wind was whipping up into a real storm.

Suddenly he heard a sound that was like no sound he had ever heard before—

It was the *Ocean*. The Great Ocean that Little Toot had never seen. And the noise came from the waves as they dashed and pounded against the rocks.

But that wasn't all. Against the black sky climbed a . . .

. . . brilliant, flaming rocket.

When Little Toot looked hard, he saw, jammed between two huge rocks, an ocean liner which his father had towed many times up and down the river.

It was truly a terrible thing to see . . .

Little Toot went wild with excitement! He began puffing those silly balls of smoke out of his smokestack . . .

And as he did, a wonderful thought struck him. Why, those smoke balls could probably be seen 'way up the river, where his father and grandfather were.

So he puffed a signal, thus . . .

'Way up the river they saw it . . .

Of course they had no idea who was making the signals, but they knew it meant "come quickly." So they all dropped what they were doing to race to the rescue.

Out from many wharves steamed a great fleet—big boats, little boats, fat ones, and skinny ones . . .

. . . With Big Toot himself right in the lead, like an admiral at the head of his fleet . . .

Just in time, too, because Little Toot, still puffing out his S.O.S., was hard put to it to stay afloat.

One wave spun him around till he was dizzy; and another tossed him up so high he was glad when a spiral-shaped wave came along for him to glide down on . . .

Before he could spit the salt water out of his smokestack, still another wave came along and tossed him up again . . .

It looked as though he'd never get down.

All this was pretty awful for a tugboat that was used to the smooth water of the river. What made it terrifying was the fact that out of the corner of his eye, when he was thus hung on a wave, Little Toot saw that the fleet wasn't able to make headway against such fierce seas.

Even Grandfather Toot was bellowing he had never seen such a storm.

Little Toot was scared green . . .

Something had to be done. But all that Little Toot had ever learned to do was blow out those silly smoke balls.

Where he was, the channel was like a narrow bottle neck with the whole ocean trying to pour in at once.

That was why the fleet couldn't make any headway. The force of the seas simply swept them back . . .

Indeed, they were on the verge of giving up entirely when suddenly above the storm they heard a gay, familiar toot . . .

It was Little Toot. Not wasting his strength butting the waves as they had done. But bouncing from crest to crest, like a rubber ball. The pounding hurt like everything, but Little Toot kept right on going.

And when Big Toot looked out to sea through his binoculars, he saw the crew on the great vessel throw a line to Little Toot.

It was a wonderful thing to see. When the line was made fast, Little Toot waited for a long moment . . .

And then, when a huge wave swept under the liner, lifting it clear of the rocks, he pulled with all of his might. *The liner came free!*

The people on board began to cheer . . .

And the whole tugboat fleet insisted upon Little Toot's escorting the great boat back into the harbor.

Little Toot was a hero!

And Grandfather Toot blasted the news all over the river. Well, after that Little Toot became quite a different fellow. He even changed his tune . . .

And it is said that he can haul as big a load as his father can . . .

. . . that is, when Big Toot hasn't a very big load to haul . . .

(From *Little Toot*)

Jack and the Beanstalk

Once upon a time there was a poor widow who had an only son named Jack and a cow named Milky-White. And all they had to live on was the milk the cow gave every morning, which they carried to the market and sold. But one morning Milky-White gave no milk, and they didn't know what to do.

"What shall we do, what shall we do?" cried the widow, wringing her hands.

"Cheer up, mother, I'll go and get work somewhere," said Jack.

"We've tried that before, and nobody would take you," said his mother. "We must sell Milky-White and with the money start a shop or something."

"All right, mother," said Jack. "It's market day today. I'll soon sell Milky-White, and then we'll see what we can do."

So he took the cow's halter in his hand and off he started. He hadn't gone far when he met a funny-looking old man who said to him, "Good morning, Jack."

"Good morning to you," said Jack, wondering how the man knew his name.

"Well, Jack, where are you off to?" asked the man.

"I'm going to the market to sell our cow."

"Oh, you look the proper sort of chap to sell cows," said the man. "I wonder if you know how many beans make five?"

"Two in each hand and one in your mouth," said Jack, as sharp as a needle.

"Right you are," said the man. "And here they are, the very beans themselves," he went on, pulling out of his pocket a number of strange-looking beans. "As you are so sharp," said he, "I don't mind doing a swop with you— your cow for these beans."

"Go along," says Jack; "wouldn't you like that!"

"Ah! you don't know what these beans are," said the man. "If you plant them tonight, by morning they will grow right up to the sky."

"Really?" said Jack. "You don't say so."

"Yes, that is so. And if it doesn't turn out to be true, you can have your cow back."

"Right," said Jack, handing him Milky-White's halter and pocketing the beans.

As Jack hadn't gone very far, it wasn't even dusk by the time he got to his door.

"Back already, Jack?" said his mother. "I see you haven't got Milky-White, so you've sold her. How much did you get for her?"

"You'll never guess, mother," said Jack.

"What was it? Five pounds, ten, fifteen? No, it can't be twenty."

"I knew you couldn't guess. What do you say to these beans? They're magical, plant them tonight and—"

"What!" cried Jack's mother, "Have you been such a fool, such an idiot, as to give away my Milky-White for these beans? Take that! Take that! Take that! And as for your precious beans, here they go out the window! Now off with you to bed. There'll be no supper for you tonight."

So Jack went upstairs to his little room in the attic, a sad and sorry boy.

When Jack woke up, the room looked very strange. The sun was shining into part of it, yet all the rest was quite dark and shady. So Jack jumped up and dressed himself and went to the window. And what do you think he saw? Why, the beans his mother had thrown out of the window into the garden had sprung up into a big beanstalk that went up and up and up till it reached the sky! So the man spoke truth after all.

The beanstalk grew quite close to Jack's window. All he had to do was open the window and jump on to the beanstalk, which ran up just like a big ladder.

Jack climbed and climbed and climbed till at last he reached the sky. And when he got there he found a long, broad road going as straight as an arrow. So he walked along the road till he came to a great big tall house. And on the doorstep there was a great big tall woman.

"Good morning, mum," said Jack, politely. "Could you be so kind as to give me some breakfast?"

"It's breakfast you want, is it?" cried the great big tall woman. "It's breakfast you'll be if you don't move off from here. My man is an Ogre, and there's nothing he likes better than boys broiled on toast."

"Oh! please mum, do give me something to eat. I've had nothing to eat since yesterday morning, really and truly, mum."

Well, the Ogre's wife was not half as bad as she looked or sounded. So she took Jack into the kitchen and gave him some bread and cheese and a jug of milk. But Jack hadn't half finished when he heard a great **thump! thump! thump!** and the whole house began to tremble.

"Goodness gracious me! It's my old man," said the Ogre's wife. "What on earth shall I do? Come along quick and jump in here." And she bundled Jack into the oven just as the Ogre came in.

He was a big one, to be sure. At his belt he had three calves strung up by the heels. He unhooked them and threw them down on the table and said: "Here, wife, fix me these for breakfast. Ah, what's this I smell?

> *Fee-fi-fo-fum,*
> *I smell the blood of an Englishman.*
> *Be he alive, or be he dead,*
> *I'll have his bones to grind my bread."*

"Nonsense, dear," said his wife, "you're dreaming. Or perhaps you smell the scraps of that little boy you had for yesterday's dinner. Go and wash, and by the time you come back your breakfast'll be ready for you."

So off the Ogre went. Jack was just going to jump out of the oven and run away when the woman told him to stay. "Wait till he's asleep," she said. "He always has a nap after breakfast."

After breakfast, the Ogre went to a big chest and took out a couple of bags of gold. He sat down and began to count, till at last his head started to nod and he began to snore till the whole house shook.

Then Jack crept out of the oven. Taking one of the bags of gold, he ran until he came to the beanstalk. Then he threw down the bag of gold into his mother's garden and climbed down and down till at last he got home. He showed his mother the gold and said, "Well, mother, wasn't I right about the beans? They are really magical, you see."

They lived on the gold for some time, but at last it

came to an end. So Jack made up his mind to try his luck once more up at the top of the beanstalk.

One fine morning he rose early and climbed and climbed and climbed till at last he came out to the road again and walked up it to the great big tall house. There, sure enough, was the great big tall woman standing on the doorstep.

"Good morning, mum," said Jack, as bold as brass. "Could you be so good as to give me something to eat?"

"Go away, my boy," said the big tall woman, "or else my man will eat you for breakfast. But aren't you the lad who came here once before? Do you know that very day my man missed one of his bags of gold?"

"That's strange, mum," said Jack, "I dare say I could tell you something about that, but I'm so hungry I can't speak till I've had something to eat."

Well the big tall woman was so curious that she took Jack in and gave him something to eat. But he had scarcely begun munching it as slowly as he could when **thump! thump! thump!** they heard the giant's footsteps. "Into the oven with you!" cried the Ogre's wife. "You can tell me about the gold when he goes to sleep." In came the Ogre, with three great oxen tied to his belt.

Throwing them down, he began to sniff the air.

> "Fee-fi-fo-fum,
> I smell the blood of an Englishman.
> Be he alive, or be he dead,
> I'll have his bones to grind my bread."

"Nonsense, dear," said his wife. "It's only the bones of the boy you ate last week. They are still in the garbage."

"Humph! Well, broil these oxen over the fire and I'll have breakfast." After he had eaten, the Ogre said, "Wife, bring me the hen that lays the golden eggs." So she brought the hen and the Ogre said: "Lay," and it laid an egg all of gold. And then the Ogre began to nod his head and snore till the house shook.

Then Jack crept out of the oven, caught hold of the golden hen, and was off before you could say "Jack Robinson." But the hen gave a cackle which woke the Ogre. Just as Jack got out of the house, he heard him calling: "Wife, what have you done with my golden hen?"

But that was all Jack heard, for he rushed to the beanstalk and climbed down like a house on fire. When he got home, he showed his mother the wonderful hen, and said "Lay." And it laid a golden egg every time he said "Lay."

Well, it wasn't long before Jack determined to have another try at his luck. So one fine morning, he rose early, got on to the beanstalk, and climbed and climbed and climbed till he got to the top. But this time he knew better than to go straight to the Ogre's house. When he got near it, he waited behind a bush till he saw the Ogre's wife come out with a pail to get some water. Jack then crept into the house and hid in a huge copper pot. He hadn't been there long when he heard **thump! thump! thump!** as before, and in came the Ogre and his wife.

"Fee-fi-fo-fum, I smell the blood of an Englishman," cried the Ogre. "I smell him, wife, I smell him."

"Do you, dearie?" said the Ogre's wife. "If it's that little rascal who stole your gold and the hen that laid the golden eggs, he's sure to be in the oven." And they both rushed to the oven. But Jack wasn't there, luckily, and the Ogre's wife said, "There you go again with your 'fee-fi-fo-fum.' Why of course it's the boy you caught last night that I've just broiled for your breakfast."

So the Ogre sat down to breakfast, but every now and then he would mutter, "Well, I could have sworn—"and he'd get up and search the cupboards. Luckily, he didn't think of the copper pot.

After breakfast was over, the Ogre called out, "Wife, wife, bring me my golden harp." So she brought out the little harp and put it on the table before him. Then he said: "Sing!" and the tiny golden harp sang most beautifully. And it went on singing till the Ogre fell asleep, and commenced to snore like thunder.

Then Jack very quietly lifted up the lid of the big pot, and got out like a mouse, and crept on hands and knees till he came to the table. He crawled up until he could reach the golden harp. Then he dropped to the floor and, holding the harp under his arm, dashed towards the door. But the harp called out, "Master! Master!" and the Ogre woke up just in time to see Jack running off with his harp.

Jack ran as fast as he could, and the Ogre came rushing after him. When Jack got to the beanstalk, he began to climb down for dear life. Well, the Ogre didn't like trusting himself to such a ladder. While he stood there, Jack got another start.

But just then the harp cried out: "Master! Master!" and the Ogre swung himself down on to the beanstalk, which shook with his weight. By this time Jack had climbed down till he was nearly home. So he called out, "Mother! Mother! Bring me the ax, bring me the ax." And his mother came rushing out with the ax in her hand.

Jack jumped down, took the ax, and gave a chop at the beanstalk. The Ogre felt the beanstalk shake and quiver. Then Jack gave another chop with the ax, and the beanstalk began to topple over. Then the Ogre fell down and broke his crown, and the beanstalk came toppling after.

What with showing the people the singing harp, and selling the golden eggs that the hen laid, Jack and his mother soon became very rich. Jack then married a beautiful princess and they lived happily ever after.

This is the house that Jack built.

THE HOUSE THAT JACK BUILT

This is the malt
That lay in the house that Jack built.
This is the rat,
That ate the malt
That lay in the house that Jack built.
This is the cat,
That killed the rat,
That ate the malt
That lay in the house that Jack built.

This is the dog,
That worried the cat,
That killed the rat,
That ate the malt
That lay in the house that Jack built.
This is the cow with the crumpled horn,
That tossed the dog,
That worried the cat,
That killed the rat,
That ate the malt
That lay in the house that Jack built.
This is the maiden all forlorn,
That milked the cow with the crumpled horn,
That tossed the dog,
That worried the cat,
That killed the rat,
That ate the malt
That lay in the house that Jack built.

This is the man all tattered and torn,
That kissed the maiden all forlorn,
That milked the cow with the crumpled horn,
That tossed the dog,
That worried the cat,

That killed the rat,
That ate the malt
That lay in the house that Jack built.
This is the priest all shaven and shorn,
That married the man all tattered and torn,
That kissed the maiden all forlorn,
That milked the cow with the crumpled horn,
That tossed the dog,
That worried the cat,
That killed the rat,
That ate the malt
That lay in the house that Jack built.

This is the cock that crowed in the morn,
That waked the priest all shaven and shorn,
That married the man all tattered and torn,
That kissed the maiden all forlorn,
That milked the cow with the crumpled horn,
That tossed the dog,
That worried the cat,
That killed the rat,
That ate the malt
That lay in the house that Jack built.

This is the farmer sowing his corn,
That kept the cock that crowed in the morn,
That waked the priest all shaven and shorn,
That married the man all tattered and torn,
That kissed the maiden all forlorn,
That milked the cow with the crumpled horn,
That tossed the dog,
That worried the cat,
That killed the rat,
That ate the malt
That lay in the house that Jack built.

(From *Mother Goose*)

THE TURNIP

Told by Alexei Tolstoi

Once upon a time an old man planted a little turnip and said:
"Grow, grow, little turnip, grow sweet! Grow, grow, little
turnip, grow strong!"

And the turnip grew up sweet and strong and big and enormous.

Then, one day, the old man went to pull it up. He pulled and
pulled again, but he could not pull it up.

He called the old woman.

The old woman pulled the old man,

The old man pulled the turnip.

And they pulled and pulled again, but they could not pull
it up.

So the old woman called her granddaughter.

The granddaughter pulled the old woman,

The old woman pulled the old man,

The old man pulled the turnip.

And they pulled and pulled again, but they could not pull
it up.

The granddaughter called the black dog.

The black dog pulled the granddaughter,

The granddaughter pulled the old woman,

The old woman pulled the old man,

The old man pulled the turnip.

And they pulled and pulled again,
but they could not pull it up.

The black dog called the cat.
The cat pulled the dog,
The dog pulled the granddaughter,
The granddaughter pulled the old woman,
The old woman pulled the old man,
The old man pulled the turnip.
And they pulled and pulled again, but still they could not
pull it up.

The cat called the mouse.
The mouse pulled the cat,
The cat pulled the dog,
The dog pulled the granddaughter,
The granddaughter pulled the old woman,
The old woman pulled the old man,
The old man pulled the turnip.
They pulled and pulled again,
and up came the turnip at last.

(From *Russian Tales for Children*)

THE PANCAKE

Retold by George Webbe Dasent

Once upon a time there was a good woman who had seven hungry children, and she was frying a pancake for them.

It was a sweet-milk pancake, and there it lay in the pan bubbling and frizzling so thick and good, it was a sight for sore eyes to look at. And the children stood round about, and the goodman sat by and looked on.

"Oh, give me a bit of pancake, Mother, dear; I am so hungry," said one child.

"Oh, darling Mother," said the second.

"Oh, darling, good Mother," said the third.

"Oh, darling, good, nice Mother," said the fourth.

"Oh, darling, pretty, good, nice Mother," said the fifth.

"Oh, darling, pretty, good, nice, clever Mother," said the sixth.

"Oh, darling, pretty, good, nice, clever, sweet Mother," said the seventh.

So they begged for the pancake all round, the one more
prettily than the other, for they
were so hungry.

"Yes, yes, children, only wait
a bit till the pancake turns itself"—she ought to have said,
"till I can get it turned"—"and
then you shall have some—a
lovely sweet-milk pancake. Only
look how fat and happy it lies
there."

When the pancake heard that,
it got afraid, and in a trice it
turned itself all of itself, and
tried to jump out of the pan, but
dropped back into it again
t'other side up. And so when it

had been fried a little on the other side too, till it got firmer in its flesh, it sprang out on the floor, and rolled off like a wheel through the door and down the hill.

"Holloa! Stop, pancake!" and away went the good woman after it, with the frying pan in one hand and the ladle in the other, as fast as she could, and her children behind her, while the good-man limped after them last of all.

"Hi! Won't you stop? Seize it. Stop, pancake," they all screamed out, one after the other, and tried to catch it on the run and hold it. But the pancake rolled on and on, and in the twinkling of an eye it was so far ahead that they couldn't see it, for the pancake was faster than any of them.

So when it had rolled awhile it met a man.

"Good day, pancake," said the man.

"God bless you, Manny Panny!" said the pancake.

"Dear pancake," said the man, "don't roll so fast. Stop a little and let me eat you."

"When I have given the slip to Goody Poody, and the good-man, and seven squalling children, I may well slip through your fingers, Manny Panny," said the pancake, and rolled on and on till it met a hen.

"Good day, pancake," said the hen.

"The same to you, Henny Penny," said the pancake.

"Pancake, dear, don't roll so fast. Bide a bit and let me eat you up," said the hen.

"When I have given the slip to Goody Poody, and the good-man, and seven squalling children, and Manny Panny, I may well slip through your claws, Henny Penny," said the pancake, and so it rolled on like a wheel down the road.

Just then it met a cock.

"Good day, pancake," said the cock.

"The same to you, Cocky Locky," said the pancake.

"Pancake, dear, don't roll so fast, but bide a bit and let me eat you up."

"When I have given the slip to Goody Poody, and the good-man, and seven squalling children, and to Manny Panny, and

Henny Penny, I may well slip through your claws, Cocky Locky," said the pancake, and off it set rolling away as fast as it could. And when it had rolled a long way it met a duck.

"Good day, pancake," said the duck.

"The same to you, Ducky Lucky."

"Pancake, dear, don't roll away so fast. Bide a bit and let me eat you up."

"When I have given the slip to Goody Poody, and the good-man, and seven squalling children, and Manny Panny, and Henny Penny, and Cocky Locky, I may well slip through your fingers, Ducky Lucky," said the pancake. With that it rolled faster than ever; and when it had rolled a long, long while, it met a goose.

"Good day, pancake," said the goose.

"The same to you, Goosey Poosey."

"Pancake, dear, don't roll so fast. Bide a bit and let me eat you up."

"When I have given the slip to Goody Poody, and the good-man, and seven squalling children, and Manny Panny, and Henny Penny, and Cocky Locky, and Ducky Lucky, I can well slip through your feet, Goosey Poosey," said the pancake, and off it rolled.

So when it rolled a long, long way farther, it met a gander.

"Good day, pancake," said the gander.

"The same to you, Gander Pander," said the pancake.

"Pancake, dear, don't roll so fast. Bide a bit and let me eat you up."

"When I have given the slip to Goody Poody, and the good-man, and seven squalling children, and Manny Panny, and Henny Penny, and Cocky Locky, and Ducky Lucky, and Goosey Poosey, I may well slip through your feet, Gander Pander," said the pancake, which rolled off as fast as ever.

So when it had rolled a long, long time, it met a pig.

"Good day, pancake," said the pig.

"The same to you, Piggy Wiggy," said the pancake, which, without a word more, began to roll and roll like mad.

"Nay, nay," said the pig, "you needn't be in such a hurry. We two can go side by side and see each other over the wood. They say it is not too safe in there."

The pancake thought there might be something in that, and so they kept company. When they had gone a short distance, they came to a brook. As for Piggy, he was so fat he swam safely across; it was nothing to him. But the poor pancake couldn't get over.

"Seat yourself on my snout," said the pig, "and I'll carry you over."

So the pancake did that.

"Ouf, ouf," said the pig, and swallowed the pancake at one gulp. And then, as the poor pancake could go no farther, why— this story can go no farther either.

(Old Norse Folk Tale)

THE FAST SOONER HOUND

A railroad man was walking down the street with his hands in his overall pockets, and a long-legged, lop-eared hound trotted behind him. The man was smoking a pipe. After a while he stopped walking, took the pipe out of his mouth and turned to the hound.

"Well, Sooner," he said, "here's the place."

They had come to a small building near the railroad tracks. Over the front door was a sign which said *Roadmaster*. The dog called Sooner didn't seem to pay much attention to the man's words; but when the man opened the door, the hound followed him inside.

The man in the office looked up from his desk. "What do you want?" he asked.

"I'm a Boomer fireman," the railroad man said, "and I'm looking for a job."

"So you're a Boomer! Well, I know what that means. You go from one railroad to another."

"That's right," the man in overalls answered proudly. "Last year I shoveled coal on the Katy. Before that I worked for the Frisco line. Before that it was the Wabash. I travel light, I travel far, and I don't let any grass grow under my feet."

"We might be able to use you on one of our trains," said the Roadmaster. "Have you got some place you can leave the dog?"

"Leave my dog!" cried the Boomer, knocking the ashes out of his pipe. "Listen here, Mr. Roadmaster, that Sooner always goes along with me."

"He does, eh? And why do you call him a Sooner?"

"He'd sooner run than eat—that's why. I raised him from a pup, and he ain't ever spent a night or a day or even an hour away from me. He'd cry fit to break his heart if we weren't

By Arna Bontemps and Jack Conroy

together. He'd cry so loud you couldn't hear yourself think."

"I don't see how I can give you a job with the hound," the Roadmaster said. "It's against the rules of the railroad to allow a passenger in the cab. Makes no difference if it's man or beast, nobody is allowed to ride with the fireman and the engineer in the cab, and no passenger is allowed in the caboose. That's Rule Number One on this road, and it's never been broken yet. What's more, it never will be broken as long as I'm Roadmaster. So it looks as if that Sooner is going to spoil things for you."

"Why, he ain't no trouble," said the Boomer. "He don't have to ride in the cab. He just runs alongside the train. When I'm on a freight train, he chases around a little in the fields to pass the time away. Sometimes he scares up a rabbit—just to play with when things get dull. But he ain't no trouble to nobody, and he never rides in the cab or the caboose."

"You mean that old hungry-looking hound can out-run a freight train?" The Roadmaster laughed. "You can't make me believe that!"

"Shucks—he'll do it without half trying," said the Boomer proudly. "Matter of fact, it will be a little bit tiresome on him having to travel so slow, but that Sooner will put up with anything just to stay close by me. He loves me that much."

"Oh, come now," said the Roadmaster. "The dog isn't born that can out-run one of our freight trains. We run the fastest freights from coast to coast. That's why we get so much business. I'm sorry we can't give you a job. You look like a man that could keep a boiler popping off on an uphill grade, but I just don't see how we can work it with the hound."

"Listen," said the Boomer. "I'll lay my first pay check against a dollar bill that my Sooner will run circles around your freight train. What's more, he'll be as fresh as a daisy when we pull into the junction, and his tongue won't even be hanging out. Of course, he'll want to trot around the station about a hundred times before we start—just to limber up, you know."

"It's a bet," said the Roadmaster, "and you can have the job. I'm not a mean man, you know, but Rule One has got to stick."

So the Boomer fireman climbed into a cab beside the engineer and began to shovel coal for all he was worth. The freight train pulled out of the station and started to pick up speed. The Sooner loped along beside it. In no time at all he had left the freight train far behind. Sometimes he would pop out of sight in the underbrush along the tracks in search of rabbits or squirrels. But before long he could be seen up ahead, waiting for the train to catch up. Once the Boomer looked out of the cab and saw a strange look on the hound's face. The Engineer noticed it too.

"What's the matter with your Sooner?" the Engineer asked. "He looks worried."

"That's right," the Boomer said. "He's worried about the hog law. That's the law that says we can't work more than sixteen hours on this run. If that happens we'll have to stop the train in the middle of the fields and wait for a fresh crew to take our places. I reckon the Sooner thinks we're going to get in trouble running so slow."

"Why, this ain't slow!" exclaimed the Engineer. "This engine is doing all it can. The boiler is hot enough to pop."

"Well, it ain't no speed for my Sooner," the Boomer laughed.

The freight train made its run and then returned, but the Sooner led it all the way. And when the dog trotted into the Roadmaster's office a mile ahead of the train, the Roadmaster got angry. He knew right away that he had lost his bet, but he didn't mind that. What he minded was what people would say about a freight train that couldn't keep up with a long-legged, lop-eared Sooner hound. They would say the train wasn't any good. The Roadmaster couldn't put up with such talk as that. No, sir. His freight trains must keep the name of being the fastest in the country.

"Look here, Boomer," he said, as the fireman climbed down from the cab. "You won the bet. That Sooner out-ran the freight train, but I'm going to transfer you to a local passenger run. What do you think about that?"

"Suits me," said the Boomer. "Me and my Sooner ain't choicy. We take the jobs we get, and we always stay together."

"You think the hound can keep up with our passenger train?"

"He'll do it easy," said the Boomer. "No trouble at all."

"If he beats our local, there'll be two dollars waiting for you when you get back. That Sooner is faster than he looks, but I don't believe he can beat a passenger train."

So the race was on again. The Sooner speeded up to a trot as they pulled out of the station, and it seemed for a while that the passenger train might get ahead of him. But just as the race was getting exciting, the local train had to stop to pick up passengers. The Sooner had to run around in the fields so he wouldn't get too far ahead of the engine. Even so, he won the race, and came into the station ten minutes ahead of the local passenger train.

The Roadmaster thought that maybe the stops were to blame for the local not keeping up with the Sooner hound.

The next time he put the Boomer in the cab of a limited passenger train that didn't make any stops till it got to the end of the line. So another race was on.

By that time people who lived along the railroad tracks were getting interested in the races. They came out of their houses to see the old mangy, no-good Sooner hound that could out-run the trains and still come into the station without his tongue hanging out an inch, and without panting the least bit. They began to think that something was surely wrong with the trains, but the trains were really right on schedule. They were keeping up their best speed.

The trouble was with that old Sooner. He ran so fast he made the trains seem slow. He did it so easily you wouldn't think he was getting anywhere until you saw him pull away from the trains. But you couldn't tell that to the country people. They felt sure the trains were slowing down. They began to talk about not riding on them any more.

"Why," they said, "passengers might just as well walk. They could get there just as fast. Those trains are too slow to talk about. If you shipped a yearling calf to market on one of them, he'd be a grown-up beef by the time he got there."

When the Roadmaster heard that kind of talk, he got mad enough to bite the heads off nails. It would have to stop. Why, that old lop-eared Sooner was spoiling everything for the railroad. The people wouldn't ride the trains, and they were sending all their freight by trucks. The Roadmaster had half a mind to fire the Boomer and tell him to take his hound and go somewhere else, but he hated to own he was licked. He was a stubborn man, and he didn't want to admit that the Sooner was just too fast for his trains.

"Hey, Boomer," he said one day, as the fireman climbed down from the cab at the end of a run. "That Sooner of yours is causing this road a lot of trouble. That no-good hound makes our trains look like snails."

"It ain't my Sooner that causes the trouble," said the Boomer. "It's that Rule Number One. My dog don't aim to give the road a black eye by out-running the trains. He just aims to stay near me, that's all. Do away with the rule and let him ride with me in the cab, and everything will be O.K."

"Not on your life. That's the oldest rule on this road, and I don't plan to change it on account of an old mangy lop-eared Sooner hound."

The Boomer shrugged his shoulders as he turned to walk away. "It's your railroad, Mr. Roadmaster," he said. Then he reached down and patted the Sooner's head. "Don't look ashamed, Sooner," he told his hound. "It ain't your fault at all."

Before the Boomer and the hound were out of sight, the Roadmaster had a fine idea. "I'll fix that Sooner," he said, snapping his fingers. "I've got what it takes to beat him. I'll put the Boomer in the cab of our Cannon Ball. That's the fastest thing on wheels. The Sooner hound is about the fastest thing on four legs, but if the fastest thing on four legs can beat the fastest thing on wheels, I'll admire to see it. That Sooner will be left so far behind it'll take a dollar to send him a postcard."

"You're going to a lot of trouble," the Boomer said to the Roadmaster, when he heard the plan. "There's no use for all this fuss. Just let my dog ride in the cab with me. That's all he wants, and it's all I want."

But the Roadmaster wouldn't change his plan. He was so sure the Cannon Ball would leave the Sooner far behind that he smiled from ear to ear.

"I aim to see this race from the cab myself," he said, "but if that Sooner beats the Cannon Ball, I'll walk back, and he can have my seat."

Word got around that the Sooner was going to try to keep up with the Cannon Ball. Farmers left off plowing, hitched up and drove to the railroad crossings to see the sight. The children were dismissed from school. So many men left the towns to see the race the factories had to close down. It was like circus day, or the county fair.

Just before the starting whistle blew, the Roadmaster climbed into the cab of the Cannon Ball with the Boomer and the Engineer. He wanted to be sure that the Boomer shoveled plenty of coal and that the Engineer kept the fast train moving at top speed. He also wanted to be close at hand to laugh at the Boomer when the Cannon Ball pulled away from the old lop-eared Sooner.

A clear track for a hundred miles was ordered for the Cannon Ball, and all the switches were spiked down. The train pulled out of the station like a streak of lightning. It took three men to see the Cannon Ball pass on that run: one to say, "There she comes," one to say, "Here she is," and another to say, "There she goes." You couldn't see a thing for steam, cinders, and smoke. The rails sang like a violin for half an hour after she had passed into the next county.

Every valve was popping off. The wheels rose three feet in the air above the roadbed. The Boomer shoveled coal for all he was worth, but he worked with a smile on his face. He knew his hound, and he didn't mind giving the dog a good run. He worked so hard he wore the hinges off the fire door. He wore the shovel down to a nub. He sweated so hard his socks got soaking wet in his shoes.

The Roadmaster stuck his head out of the cab window. *Whoosh!* Off went his hat—and he nearly lost his head too.

Gravel pinged against his goggles like hailstones. He peered through the smoke and steam. Where was the Sooner? The Roadmaster couldn't see hide nor hair of him anywhere. He let out a whoop of joy.

"The SOONER! The SOONER!" he yelled. "He's *nowhere* in sight! This is the time we out-ran that old lop-eared hound."

"I can't understand that," the Boomer said. "That Sooner ain't never failed me before. It just ain't like him to lay down on me. Let me take a look."

He dropped his shovel and poked his head out of the window. He looked far and wide. The Roadmaster was right. The Sooner was nowhere to be seen. Where could he be?

The Roadmaster kept poking fun at the Boomer and laughing

all the rest of the way to the station. But the Boomer didn't answer. Every moment or two he'd glance out of the window. Surely something was wrong. What had become of his Sooner?

Presently the station came into sight, and the Cannon Ball began to slow down.

A moment later the Boomer saw a great crowd of people around the station. He supposed they were waiting to greet the Cannon Ball and to give it a cheer for making such a fast run. But no, they weren't even looking down the tracks. They were all watching something else.

"Those people aren't even noticing us," the Roadmaster said

to the Engineer. "Blow the whistle."

The Engineer blew the whistle just before he brought the Cannon Ball to a stop. Still nobody paid any attention. The people were all looking the other way and laughing. The Boomer and the Roadmaster and the Engineer were all puzzled. They climbed down out of the cab.

"Well, here we are!" the Roadmaster cried, trying to get some attention. Nobody gave him any, so he pushed his way through the crowd. "What's going on here?" he insisted. "Didn't you people come down here to see the Cannon Ball?"

"Take it away," somebody answered. "It's too slow to catch cold. The Sooner's been here ten minutes and more."

The Boomer's heart gave a big jump when he heard that news. It seemed too good to be true. But a minute later he saw with his own eyes. Around the corner of the station came the old lop-eared hound, chasing a rabbit that he had rounded up along the way. He was having so much fun playing with the little creature and making the people laugh, that he had plumb forgot about the Cannon Ball.

"He's here!" the Boomer shouted. "He's here! My Sooner's true blue, and he's won again!"

The Roadmaster was so overcome he chewed up his cigar like a stick of chewing gum and swallowed it. "P-p-put him in the cab," he sputtered. "P-p-put him in the cab and get going."

"But where will *you* sit?" The Boomer asked with a grin.

"I'll walk," the Roadmaster answered, as he started chewing on a fresh cigar. "Anything to stop that hound from out-running our trains."

A few moments later the Boomer was back in the cab, his hound beside him, and the big crowd of people let out a great cheer as the Cannon Ball pulled out of the station for the home trip. The Sooner seemed to know whom the cheer was for. There was an unmistakable smile on his face. As the train gathered speed, his long ears flapped gaily in the breeze.

Just before the station went out of sight, the three in the cab of the Cannon Ball saw a man leave the crowd and begin to walk down the tracks. It was the Roadmaster starting for home.

(From *The Fast Sooner Hound*)

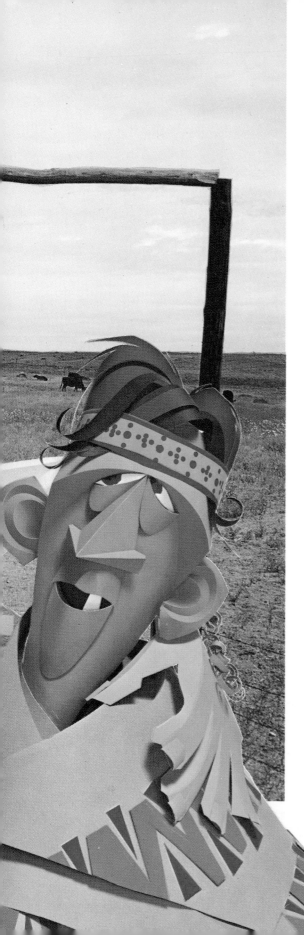

FEBOLDSON,
WESTERN SCIENTIST

By Walter Blair

Nebraska, at the start, was big enough so great hunks could be chopped off and handed over to Colorado, Dakota, and Idaho without anybody in Nebraska getting worried. After these gifts had been passed out, it was seen that every dratted mountain in the whole vicinity had been handed over to some other state. Result was that the whole of Nebraska was nothing but valleys, tableland and rolling prairies, all with a southwestern exposure. This meant that all the weather and all the wild life that came along had plenty of room to work and play in without natural let or hindrance.

Febold Feboldson settled down out there about the time the weather began to feel its strength. He got his farm and his family started, took on the job of Indian Agent for the Dirtyleg Indians, and then started his great work as a natural scientist.

One of the first things he had to cope with was the Great Fog that came along the year of the Great Heat. The Great Heat was bad enough, Heaven knows. Looking back, many people said that one of the most fiendish things about it was the way the mercury in thermometers everywhere shot up the tubes and spewed out the top like a fountain, so people couldn't *tell* how hot it was. Over in Saline County, though, one fellow with a big thermometer that'd take two hundred and thirty-two degrees, stood by it day and night with a cake of ice, bound and determined to save his thermometer. And he said the heat never went below a hundred and fifty degrees all those weeks, leastwise when he could see the thermometer with the help of either the sun, the moon or a lantern.

That was bad enough, as you can imagine. But one day Febold looked at the sky, fiddled around with some of his instruments, and made a horrible discovery. "That's bad," he said. "Got to do something drastic."

What he did was send a cable to London that read this way: "Send along a gross of your fanciest fog-cutters soon as possible, C.O.D. Febold Feboldson."

Being a scientist, you see, Febold had figured out right away what a horrible time Nebraska was in for. He told Mrs. Feboldson about the steps he'd taken that very evening while they were sitting in the sitting room trying to cool off a bit.

"Cabled over to London today for a gross of fog-cutters," he said.

Mrs. Feboldson's eyes stuck out so far they appeared to be on stems. "Fog-cutters?" she said, dazed-like.

"Yes, fog-cutters, Mother," he said. "You see, they have the thickest fogs in London that they have anywhere except on the ocean. And they're inventive there, you know—a right smart race. So they've doubtless got the best fog-cutters you can find anywhere."

"Of course, Febold, but I can't see as we need any fog-cutters. What would we do with them?"

"Cut the fog."

"It's been hot enough to make me wish we could cut the heat," says Mrs. Feboldson. "But if you look out the window there, you'll notice there's no fog—nothing but level land and sky, as far as you can look, with a hundred thousand heat waves, just what you usually see out that living room window."

"Some unusual things out there, too," says Febold. "What's that dark gray thing up in the sky yonder—a dark gray thing no bigger than a man's hand?"

"Why!" Mrs. Feboldson said. "It's a cloud—first one I've seen since the Great Heat started pestering us. Looks as if it might be a rain cloud."

Febold nodded. "How about that little toe of yours that warns you when we're to have rain? How's it feel?"

Mrs. Feboldson noticed her toe for a minute, then, "I'll swan, it's a-twitching," she told him.

"I've fiddled around with my barometers, looked at the moon, and listened to the bullfrogs, and they all say the same thing," Febold said. "What's more, they say it's going to be a regular Bible storm—forty days and forty nights. Oh, we'll need those fog-cutters all right, Mother."

"Do they cut rain as well as fogs?"

"No, they just cut fogs, I reckon. But we'll need them. You'll see. Let's turn in."

Along toward morning, there was the beginning of that horrible sound that people in Nebraska (and parts of the neighboring territories) kept nearly being driven crazy by for the next forty days and forty nights. People that tried to describe it later said it was like the sound of steam shooting out of three million tea-kettles at once—big kettles, too, boiling like fury—just one long burbling hiss.

As soon as Febold came in from milking, Mrs. Feboldson asked him what that horrible noise was.

"It's working the way I figured it would," he said. "The rain's coming down like a dribbled ocean. But up there ten miles or so, it's spattering down on the hot air that was piled up around here by the Great Heat. As soon as the rain hits the hot air, it turns to steam and makes that hissing noise. The steam will be the fog."

"But the steam's staying up there," Mrs. Feboldson said. "Out the window, all you can see is level land and sky as far as you can look, same as usual, only gray because there's no sun today."

"Pretty soon, Mother, the rain will hammer the fog down to the ground, and what'll pile up will be the fog. Hope those Englishmen hurry up with those fog-cutters. Things are going to be bad."

Febold was right, as usual. There was a little fog at first, then more and more of it, until taking a walk alone was impossible. At least two people would be needed so one could part the fog and hold it apart while the other one walked through. Cattle didn't have to be watered, because they could drink the fog. But the dirt farmers were scared speechless, because their crops were in a bad way. You see, some of the seeds had figured that the closest sunshine was in China, and had started growing downward.

Around Thanksgiving, when the fog was so thick that portions had turned to three hundred thousand gallons of slush, both farmers and stockmen by the hundreds had about decided to pull out of Nebraska. "Too crowded by this danged fog," they said. "We need elbow room."

It was when things had come to this kind of a pass that the fog-cutters arrived, C.O.D. Febold used one of them to cut red tape so he could pay for them out of his Dirtyleg Indian fund. Then he started to use them on the fog—to slice it into big neat strips. Soon, when he had great piles of these strips, it was needful that he figure out where to put them.

"Can't leave them lying out there on the fields," he told Mrs. Feboldson, "or all the seeds will keep growing downward. I know! I'll lay them out along the roads."

Upshot was that he put those fog strips end to end all along the dirt roads of Nebraska. And before long some of the slush-fog seeped down, and some got so covered with dust that nobody could see where Febold had buried the Great Fog.

Only one serious bad result came of the whole thing. Every spring, when the sun begins to shine and the thaw comes, some of this old fog seeps up on the dirt roads, turning them into the gooiest mess you ever got stuck in.

And if you don't believe this, just go out to Nebraska some spring and try driving on one of those roads.

(From *Tall Tale America*)

How They Bring Back The Village Of Cream Puffs When the Wind Blows It Away

By Carl Sandburg

A girl named Wing Tip the Spick came to the Village of Liver-and-Onions to visit her uncle and her uncle's uncle on her mother's side and her uncle and her uncle's uncle on her father's side.

It was the first time the four uncles had a chance to see their little relation, their niece. Each one of the four uncles was proud of the blue eyes of Wing Tip the Spick.

The two uncles on her mother's side took a long deep look into her blue eyes and said, "Her eyes are so blue, such a clear light blue, they are the same as cornflowers with blue raindrops shining and dancing on silver leaves after a sun shower in any of the summer months."

And the two uncles on her father's side, after taking a long deep look into the eyes of Wing Tip the Spick, said, "Her eyes are so blue, such a clear light shining blue, they are the same as cornflowers with blue raindrops shining and dancing on the silver leaves after a sun shower in any of the summer months."

And though Wing Tip the Spick didn't listen and didn't hear what the uncles said about her blue eyes, she did say to herself when they were not listening, "I know these are sweet uncles and I am going to have a sweet time visiting my relations."

The four uncles said to her, "Will you let us ask you two questions, first the first question and second the second question?"

"I will let you ask me fifty questions this morning, fifty questions tomorrow morning, and fifty questions any morning. I like to listen to questions. They slip in one ear and slip out of the other."

Then the uncles asked her the first question first, "Where do you come from?" and the second question second, "Why do you have two freckles on your chin?"

"Answering your first question first," said Wing Tip the Spick, "I come from the Village of Cream Puffs, a little light village on the upland corn prairie. From a long ways off it looks like a little hat you could wear on the end of your thumb to keep the rain off your thumb."

"Tell us more," said one uncle. "Tell us much," said another uncle. "Tell it without stopping," added another uncle. "Interruptions nix nix," murmured the last of the uncles.

168

"It is a light little village on the upland corn prairie many miles past the sunset in the west," went on Wing Tip the Spick. "It is light the same as a cream puff is light. It sits all by itself on the big long prairie where the prairie goes up in a slope. There on the slope the winds play around the village. They sing it wind songs, summer wind songs in summer, winter wind songs in winter.

"And sometimes like an accident, the wind gets rough. And when the wind gets rough it picks up the little Village of Cream Puffs and blows it away off in the sky—all by itself."

"O-o-h-h," said one uncle. "Um-m-m-m," said the other three uncles.

"Now the people in the village all understand the winds with their wind songs in summer and winter. And they understand the rough wind who comes sometimes and picks up the village and blows it away off high in the sky all by itself.

"If you go to the public square in the middle of the village you will see a big roundhouse. If you take the top off the roundhouse you will see a big spool with a long string winding up around the spool.

"Now whenever the rough wind comes and picks up the village and blows it away off high in the sky all by itself then the string winds loose off the spool, because the village is fastened to the string. So the rough wind blows and blows and the string on the spool winds looser and looser the farther the village goes blowing away off into the sky all by itself.

"Then at last when the rough wind, so forgetful, so careless, has had all the fun it wants, then the people of the village all come together and begin to wind up the spool and bring back the village where it was before."

"O-o-h-h," said one uncle. "Um-m-m-m," said the other three uncles.

"And sometimes when you come to the village to see your little relation, your niece who has four such sweet uncles, maybe she will lead you through the middle of the city to the public square and show you the roundhouse. They call it the Roundhouse of the Big Spool. And they are proud because it was thought up and is there to show when visitors come."

"And now will you answer the second question second—why do you have two freckles on your chin?" interrupted the uncle who had said before, "Interruptions nix nix."

"The freckles are put on," answered Wing Tip the Spick. "When a girl goes away from the Village of Cream Puffs her mother puts on two freckles, on the chin. Each freckle must be the same as a little burnt cream puff kept in the oven too long. After the two freckles looking like two little burnt cream puffs are put on her chin, they remind the girl every morning when she combs her hair and looks in the looking glass. They remind her where she came from and she mustn't stay away too long."

"O-h-h-h," said one uncle. "Um-m-m-m," said the other three uncles. And they talked among each other afterward, the four uncles by themselves, saying:

"She has a gift. It is her eyes. They are so blue, such a clear light blue, the same as cornflowers with blue raindrops shining and dancing on silver leaves after a sun shower in any of the summer months."

At the same time Wing Tip the Spick was saying to herself, "I know for sure now these are sweet uncles and I am going to have a sweet time visiting my relations."

(From *Rootabaga Stories*)

SHAWNEEN AND THE GANDER

By Richard Bennett

On the top of a high green hill in Ireland there once lived a little boy and his name was Shawneen.

One bright warm day while his mother was washing out the clothes she said, "The fire is out and there isn't a match in the house. Run down to Mrs. Murphy's shop like a good lad and buy a box. Here is a penny."

Indeed there was no need for a second word about that. Shawneen was always ready to go on errands to Mrs. Murphy's.

"I will to be sure," said he, putting his cap on his head and the penny in his pocket.

Now at the foot of the hill there was a little village with a row of houses and shops up one side of the street and down the other.

Mrs. Murphy's was the prize of the lot. She sold everything. If you wanted to buy a dress or if you wanted to buy a ham Mrs. Murphy would be sure to have it.

When Shawneen arrived at her shop he was out of breath. He had been running down the hill and it was a good way round when you came by the road. Before opening the door he stopped for a minute to look in the window.

The first shelf had the usual array of cups and saucers and the second shelf had nothing on it to talk about, but on the third shelf right near the glass Shawneen saw the most beautiful bugle he had ever seen in all his life.

It glistened so brightly in the sun that Shawneen could scarcely look at it.

It was all the color of gold and so shiny he could see himself seven times in it.

When Paddy the postman walked by the window to deliver the letters seven Paddys walked by in the bugle. It was that bright. Oh, I can tell you it was lovely.

Around the middle was tied a blue-and-yellow cord with a silky tassel on each end as big as your hand.

Shawneen went into the shop.

"A box of matches if you please, ma'am," said he to Mrs. Murphy; "and if it wouldn't be asking too much may I have a toot on the bugle?"

"A toot is it?" said Mrs. Murphy. "Indeed you may, my lad, two if you like. There is no harm in a good toot."

So Mrs. Murphy took the bugle out of the window and gave it to Shawneen. The end was cold and smooth and shaped so nicely that it fit snugly over his mouth.

"Now don't be afraid of it, my lad," said Mrs. Murphy. "Give us a good blow."

Shawneen blew very gently at first, then a little louder, and then so loud you could hear it down the street and over the hill and down by the sea.

Shawneen had never heard anything so fine in all his life.

"Ah, it's grand entirely," said he, stroking the tassels. "How much is it?"

"Ah, that's a very fine bugle," said Mrs. Murphy. "I couldn't let you have it for less than ten shillings and sixpence."

Shawneen blew on the bugle again but not so loud this time, then put it back on the counter.

Ten shillings and sixpence was a lot of money. Indeed a pair of shoes would cost as much as that.

Shawneen gave Mrs. Murphy the penny and put the box of matches in his coat pocket.

He walked slowly out the door and down the street.

He was thinking very hard to himself. How could he get ten shillings and sixpence to buy the bugle in Mrs. Murphy's shop window?

There was no money at home to be spent for bugles. Indeed he was well sure of that. Didn't his mother need a new shawl and the donkey a new harness and the window a new pane of glass? Wasn't his mother's teapot badly cracked and she often saying she wished she had the price of a new one? Weren't the soles of his own shoes so thin he decided to take a short cut across the fields as the gravel on the road hurt his feet?

"No, indeed," said Shawneen to himself, "it will be no use asking for ten shillings and sixpence to buy a bugle."

He jumped over the ditch and began to climb the hedge.

The heather and moss at the top felt nice and soft so he sat down for a bit to think the matter over.

He was no sooner nicely settled when all of a sudden he saw a strange little man dressed all in green asleep under a furze bush only a few feet away. He was no more than a foot long and his suit was so much the color of the grass about him that indeed Shawneen had to look sharp to make him out at all.

"It's a Leprechaun surely," whispered Shawneen to himself, "and the very lad who can tell me how I can get ten shillings and sixpence to buy the bugle."

Before you could say two two's Shawneen had the little fellow about the waist.

Now you may be sure it isn't every day you see a Leprechaun and when you do you have to keep your eyes on him or it's off he is in no time at all.

Shawneen lifted the little maneen out from under the bush. The Leprechaun awoke with a great start and let such a yell out of him you wouldn't think he was equal to it. It was that loud.

"Ah, let me down now like a good lad," said the little fellow, kicking this way and that. "This is no way to be treating a gentleman."

"I will, faith," said Shawneen, "but first you must tell me how I can get ten shillings and sixpence to buy the bugle in Mrs. Murphy's shop window."

"Ah, that's easy enough," said the Leprechaun, "But you are hurting me now. Take your thumb off my stomach like a good lad."

Shawneen lifted his thumb a bit and then the Leprechaun began to stretch his arms and stretch his legs and rub his eyes at a great rate.

"This warm weather makes one very sleepy," said he.

"Never mind that now," said Shawneen; "how can I get ten shillings and sixpence to buy the bugle?"

"Ah, you are a very determined lad," said the Leprechaun. "Why, earn it, of course. You can't expect to get something for nothing."

"I know that well enough," said Shawneen, "but how can I earn all that money?"

The Leprechaun put one of his long bony fingers to the side of his nose and leaning forward whispered very mysteriously, "Not a word to a soul now," said he, "hatch the egg and sell the gander."

"What egg?" said Shawneen, squeezing the little fellow tighter than ever.

The Leprechaun didn't say another word but pointed to the earth.

Before Shawneen stopped to think he glanced down and there by the side of the ditch was the biggest goose egg he had ever seen in all his life.

I needn't tell you the Leprechaun was gone in a flash.

"Well, the egg is real enough, faith," said Shawneen, picking it up and putting it in his cap to keep it from breaking.

"An egg the size of this should make a big gander and a big gander should bring a good price at the Fair. I should have enough money in all to buy my mother a new shawl and a new dress and a silver teapot and still have enough left over to buy a bugle."

He was so excited he could hardly wait to get home. The

sooner the hatching began the better.

Over the fields he went, leaping the ditches and climbing the hedges. That the egg wasn't broken was nothing less than a miracle.

When he reached home his mother was hanging out the clothes.

"What have you there, my lad?" said she.

"A goose egg," said Shawneen.

"A goose egg, is it?" said his mother. "I have seen big eggs in my day but nothing the likes of that. Where did you find it?"

Now Shawneen remembered what the Leprechaun had said about keeping quiet.

"I was coming across the field," said he, "and there it was all by itself in the shelter of the ditch."

"And what will you do with an egg like that?" said his mother.

"Hatch it," said Shawneen. "Is there a hen setting?"

"There is, to be sure," said his mother. "Bring it into the shed."

She opened the hen-house door and pointed to a big brown hen nesting in one corner.

"I am afraid she will find it a bit uncomfortable," said Shawneen, pushing the hen aside a bit.

"Oh, in a few days she will be so used to it she will never know it was there at all," said his mother.

Now goodness knows the egg did make the poor hen sit a bit crooked to be sure. But she was a quiet, obliging bird and went on sitting as if nothing had happened.

There she sat with one side up and one side down for days and days, a very mountain of patience.

Every morning Shawneen took a little peek under her wing to make sure all was going well and every now and then he went to have a look at the bugle in Mrs. Murphy's shop window. The bugle seemed to grow more beautiful every day and when Mrs. Murphy let him have a little toot on it now and then it sounded richer and sweeter as the days went by.

Well, the time passed as time will and soon the eggs were hatched—twelve yellow chicks and one yellow gosling. The chicks were fluffy and pretty as you may expect, but the gosling was a sight.

I don't think you could have found an uglier bird in the length and breadth of all Ireland.

His pin feathers stuck out of him like the bristles of an old pig and his feet were so big and red and awkward he was forever stepping on his own toes.

His head was as big as a gosling twice his size and his poor little neck so thin and scrawny that it looked for all the world like a cabbage on the end of a broomstick.

"Ah, he is beautiful," said Shawneen to his mother; "may I raise him myself?"

"Indeed you may," said she. "I am sure I will have nothing to do with him. I have raised ducks and geese in my day but I have never seen anything come out of an egg the likes of that. Goodness knows what kind of a gander he will make. He has altogether too knowing a look in his eye to my notion. Faith, he looks at you as if he knew what you are thinking. Take my word the sooner you fatten him up and send him off to the Fair the better."

Shawneen thought this was a good idea. The sooner he had the money in his pocket the sooner he could buy his bugle.

So every day he fed his gander the best of this and the best of that. Shawneen thought nothing was too good for him. In no time at all the gander was as big as the hens and as big as the turkeys and soon as big as the geese themselves.

Indeed he grew so fast he became the talk of all the neighbors for lands around.

"That's no common gander," everyone began to say. "He comes from no common stock, I can tell you. Look at the way he carries himself! You would think he owned the world and all!"

Now all this talk and all this attention made the gander very proud. Oh, you have no idea. In fact, he was so carried away with himself that he would have nothing to do with the other birds of the barnyard. With the air of a king he walked before them.

The ducks thought he was very funny and laughed at him.

The hens had never seen his like before and were a bit afraid of him.

But the geese were so put about with his fine airs they couldn't stand the sight of him.

Now with the animals, it was a different story.

"Oh, he is only a gander," said they, and went on about their business. They wouldn't even look in his direction.

This didn't please the gander, you may be sure of that. Since they gave him no attention he took great delight in teasing them every chance he could get.

Pulling the pigs' tails while they were eating their supper was one of his favorite tricks.

"Faith, I will wring his neck if he goes on with any more of that," said Shawneen's father.

"Maybe he doesn't like curly tails," said Shawneen; "he was just trying to straighten them out a bit."

"Straighten them out, indeed," said his father. "I'll straighten him out in short order if he goes on with any more of that nonsense."

One day the gander made faces at the donkey and the poor little fellow was so frightened he backed the cart wheel over a boulder and upset two churns of butter and two fine baskets of eggs.

Another day he chased the goats over the young cabbages and one little patch of potatoes. You can imagine the state of the garden.

One day Shawneen's mother decided to clean out the house. She washed the windows and swept the floor and polished the pots and pans. When everything was nice and neat she went out to get a pail of water.

Meanwhile it started to rain. Over the half door flew the gander as easy as you please and made himself at home in front of the fireplace. He shook the rain off his feathers and flapped his wings, blowing the ashes and cinders all over the house.

"Oh, glory," said Shawneen's mother when she opened the door, "that bird will drive us out of house and home. I think the safest place for him is in the pot."

"Oh, no," said Shawneen, "he was just trying to be helpful and blow up the fire a bit. He is a very thoughtful gander."

"Thoughtful, indeed," said his mother. "It's a nice job he has given me with his thoughtfulness. Another trick like that and into the pot he goes."

I needn't tell you Shawneen was beginning to get worried when he heard this. The gander was acting very strange, to be sure. He would never get to the Fair at the rate he was going. But never a fear had the gander.

He made friends with all the hungry crows of the neighborhood and one evening invited them all in for supper. They ate up the grain in no time at all and the poor hens had to go to bed hungry. Oh, he was a holy terror.

There was no holding him.

Another day Shawneen's mother made some bread. She mixed the dough in a large pan and put it on the table near the fire while she hung out the clothes.

It was a warm afternoon and the gander was feeling a bit drowsy. He jumped over the half door again as familiar as you please and settled himself for a nice comfortable nap in the very middle of the pan.

"Oh, glory," said Shawneen's mother when she opened the door. "This is too much. Tomorrow is Fair day. That gander goes with your father. Whatever price he will bring he will have to go. We can't put up with him a minute longer. There is something very strange about that bird. Heaven knows what he may do to us all if he takes the notion."

"Sh, sh, sh, sh," said the gander, jumping out of the pan and leaping over the half door. He stood outside for a minute with his ear to the crack and heard the whole story. He knew very well that when ganders or geese went to the Fair they never came back. Oh, he was no fool.

That night he never slept a wink. He stood on one foot and then on the other. When the cock began to crow his mind was made up. He would hide outside the garden wall until Shawneen's father was well out of sight.

Now as luck would have it, who should be sleeping outside the garden wall that very minute but Ned the Napper—the foxiest rogue in all Ireland. He was forever sneaking up and down the countryside stealing everything he could lay his hands on.

Over the wall came the gander and landed squarely on top of his head. Feathers went flying, I can tell you. Such kicking and biting you never saw. For a while in the dim light you couldn't tell which was Ned and which was the gander. But I am sorry to say foxy Ned soon had the upper hand. He tucked the gander safely in his bag, tossed it over his shoulder and made off east the road.

That morning when Shawneen's father had hitched the donkey to the cart and was ready to be off no gander could be found. They all looked high and they all looked low but no gander could they see. They looked behind this and they looked behind that, but not a feather of him was in sight.

"Well, gander or no gander," said Shawneen's father, "I can't wait any longer." So he slapped the lines over the donkey's back and set off to the Fair.

Shawneen watched the donkey cart rattling down the lane and through the gate. Soon it turned a bend of the road and was out of sight. He stood in the middle of the road wondering what to do next. He had waited so long for the egg to hatch and for the gander to grow a bit. Indeed it was a trial keeping him out of the pot with all his strange actions. Now when he was ready for the Fair he was nowhere to be found. Shawneen couldn't help but think of the bugle in Mrs. Murphy's shop window. It was likely to stay just where it was. Shining away for itself on the top shelf.

Shawneen ate his breakfast very slowly, thinking very hard to himself.

"Perhaps he has gone for a walk," said he to his mother.

"Very likely, indeed," said she. "Faith, he was liable to do most anything."

Shawneen decided to take a walk east the road. The gander might have gone in that direction.

Now Shawneen hadn't gone very far when he met two women gathering their washing off the hedges where it had been put out to dry.

"Did you see a big gander pass by here, by any chance?" said

Shawneen.

"A gander, is it?" said one of the women very crossly. "No, indeed, but I would like to get a glimpse of the rogue that made off with my husband's new Sunday shirt and my two fine linen aprons."

Shawneen went on a little further until he came to a little cottage. Outside the door was an old woman spinning.

"Did you see a big gander pass by here by any chance?" said Shawneen.

"A gander, is it?" said the old woman. "No, my child, but I would like to get a glimpse of my little teapot I put out to dry on the windowsill. A fine, shiny little teapot it was. The fairies must have had their eyes on it."

Shawneen went on his way. Around another bend of the road he met two men cutting turf.

"Did you see a big gander pass by here, by any chance?" said Shawneen.

"A gander, is it?" said one of the men very crossly. "Indeed I didn't, but I would like to lay my hands on the rogue that made off with our coats and dinner pail when our backs were turned."

A little way further Shawneen came to a tinkers' van that was standing by the side of the road. Three of the tinkers were talking together in a very wild manner.

"Did you see a big gander pass by here by any chance?" asked Shawneen.

"A gander, is it?" said one of the tinkers very crossly. "No, I didn't, but I would like to lay my hands on the rogue that made off with our finest pots and pans."

Now a little way further Shawneen came to a crossroads where some young people were dancing on a large flat stone by the side of the ditch.

"Did you see a big gander pass by here by any chance?" cried Shawneen.

The young people were so busy laughing and dancing and the fiddler so busy playing and calling out the sets that no one paid any attention.

Shawneen said no more but walked slowly along the little road that ran up the side of a hill.

"A flock of ganders could pass by that crowd and I am sure they would be none the wiser," said Shawneen to himself. "It's too busy dancing they are."

Now he hadn't gone many steps when he met two guards.

"Did you see a big gander pass by here by any chance?" said Shawneen.

"A gander, is it?" said one of the guards. "No, my lad, but we would like to lay our hands on Ned the Napper. We heard he was around these parts."

Shawneen sat on a stone near by and wondered what to do next. His hopes of finding the gander seemed less than ever.

Now during all this time great clouds had been rolling across the sky and soon big raindrops began to fall.

"I'll be drenched surely," said Shawneen, looking about for a bit of shelter. An old ruined castle at the top of a near-by hill was the only thing in sight. He climbed over the hedge and ran up the hill. He walked quickly across the yard and through the castle door.

It was dark and gloomy among the old walls and the ivy rustled and whispered in the wind. In the far corner of the first room Shawneen found a spot that was fairly dry in spite of the wind and rain.

Now he was no sooner nicely settled when all of a sudden he heard a strange noise in the next room.

"Sh, sh, sh, sh," it went very softly.

"Sh, sh, sh, sh," it went again a little louder than before.

"Rain or no rain, I'll stay here no longer," said Shawneen, starting for the door.

"Sh, sh, sh, sh," came the noise again, a little louder this time.

Shawneen stopped a bit. He had heard that sound before.

He tiptoed gently to the door of the next room and peeked in. You can well imagine his surprise. There on the floor was a fierce-looking man fast asleep. By his side was a big bag—and what in the world should be sticking out of the side of it but the gander's head.

The man stirred in his sleep. He began to rub his nose. He was going to wake up, there was no doubt about that. Shawneen held his breath.

Just then the gander leaned over and said "Sh, sh," so softly in his ear that the man went on sleeping as sound as ever.

Then the gander began to tear the sack very slowly with his strong bill.

As the hole became bigger and bigger Shawneen suddenly remembered what the guards had said about Ned the Napper. Beyond a doubt this was the very lad the guards were after.

Without a word Shawneen tiptoed across the room. He ran out the door and down the hill. His feet splashed in all the pools and the rain blinded him so badly he could hardly see. As luck would have it the guards hadn't gone very far. Shawneen came running up puffing and blowing. He was so excited he could hardly speak.

"Up there, up there!" shouted Shawneen, pointing to the castle.

"What's up there, my lad?" said one of the guards.

"Ned the Napper, I think, sir," said Shawneen.

Without another word they all ran up the hill. Before you could say two two's the guards had the fierce-looking man safely between them.

With a few good bites the gander stepped out of the bag and gave himself a good shake. He was as cross as two sticks. And indeed it's well he may be. To be tossed into a bag like an old cabbage head would be hard on anyone's dignity.

"This is a lucky day for you, my lad," said one of the guards to Shawneen. "It will be well worth your while to come down to the barracks with us. This is Ned the Napper all right, all right. It's a long chase he has given us. We will leave his bag here and take care of that later. It will be quite safe in this deserted place."

So down the hill they went—foxy Ned with a guard on each arm and Shawneen and the gander out before.

A few minutes later Shawneen and one of the guards walked out of the barracks door. Shawneen was carrying a little leather sack in one hand. In it was enough money to buy teapots and shoes and dresses and shawls. And bugles!

"Well indeed, my lad," said the guard; "you well deserve this reward for telling us about Ned the Napper. Now that the rain is over let us go back to the castle and see what we can find in the bag."

So up the hill they went. When they reached the castle the guard turned the bag upside down.

Coats and shirts and pots and pans came tumbling out on the floor.

"Why, this must be the old lady's teapot," said Shawneen, "all wrapped up in the turfcutter's coat, and here are the women's aprons and the tinkers' pots and pans."

"Do you know who all these things belong to?" said the guard, scratching his head.

"Indeed I do," said Shawneen, rattling the money in the little sack. "It's scattered west the road they are—tinkers and turfcutters, old ones and young ones. Have a little patience now, your honor. I'll bring them all flying in short order."

Without another word he was down the hill and into Mrs.

Murphy's shop. Before you could say two two's he was out again and up the hill blowing the fine shiny bugle for all he was worth. Ah, indeed, it's fine and clear it sounded ringing out through all the countryside. Through all the lands around its like was never heard before. All who heard it came running up the hill. The tinkers, the women, the turfcutters, the dancers—even the old woman left her spinning wheel and came as far as she could to see what was making such a sweet sound. Soon they all arrived. Shawneen lined them up before the castle door. When each received his bit Shawneen blew a fine lively toot on the bugle. Then there was merry talk, you may be sure. A few minutes later they all went down the hill and west the road. The fiddler played and the young people sang and the gander strutted out before as if he owned the world and all.

"Oh, he is no common gander," everyone said. "It's easy to see that. There isn't a finer bird in the length and breadth of all Ireland."

(From *Shawneen and the Gander*)

HOW IT SNOWED FUR AND RAINED FRY CAKES IN WESTERN VIRGINIA

By Mary E. Cober

One day Tony heard that a school had been started over in the next valley. Never having been in a school, Tony was anxious to see what one looked like. Early one morning he set out to walk the twenty miles to take a look.

Tony found he liked school right well. He found that by stretching his legs a little more than usual, he could soon take some mighty big steps. Before he was through, he could take a step of almost a quarter of a mile. Along with finding a few short cuts, Tony was able to get to school in jig time.

One day when he was moseying to school, he saw two big mountain lions—he called them painters—one on each side of the path. "They'll be looking for trouble and I don't want to be it," Tony thought. Then he had an idea. "Sic'em! Sic'em!" he cried.

Immediately the two big cats flew at each other. As they tussled they kept jumping higher and higher. Soon they were jumping as high as Tony's head.

"Sic'em! Sic'em!" Tony yelled again.

This time the two painters jumped as high as the trees and fought harder than ever.

After school Tony used the same path, keeping a sharp eye out for the painters. They were not to be seen but as he drew near the place where he had seen them last, bits of fur began to float down from the sky. "That's strange," thought Tony. "Where can this be coming from?"

Tony looked all around and then saw a fleecy cloud from which the fur seemed to be coming. "Why, those painters have jumped so high that they landed in the clouds," he cried.

And that's exactly what happened. And *that's* the time it snowed fur in western Virginia.

Tony found that his trips to school resulted in many interesting experiences. One day his granny, who was visiting them for a spell, made some fry cakes, or doughnuts as you would probably call them. She made so many that even the hearty-eating Beavers couldn't finish them all. Tony took along a sack to school for the teacher.

Now on the way Tony met Brer Rabbit who had come to pay his Virginia cousins a visit. Tony was munching a doughnut and this made Brer Rabbit very hungry; so he decided to get all of the fry cakes for himself.

"Hi, Big Boy," greeted Brer Rabbit. "What you got there?"

"Fry cakes," Tony answered politely. "Have one?"

"Well, don't mind if I do. Say, I know some magic words that will make these fry cakes multiply and then there will be lots for both of us."

"What are the words?" Tony asked.

"First, you must put the fry cakes on that tree stump, and then close your eyes. After that I'll tell you the magic words."

Tony did as directed, only he didn't close his eyes tight. When he saw Brer Rabbit reach for the cakes, Tony's toe reached for Brer Rabbit and he kicked him sky high into the air. And *that's* the time it rained fry cakes for three days over all of western Virginia.

You see, even as a young'un, Tony Beaver was hard to beat.

(From *The Remarkable History of Tony Beaver, West Virginian*)

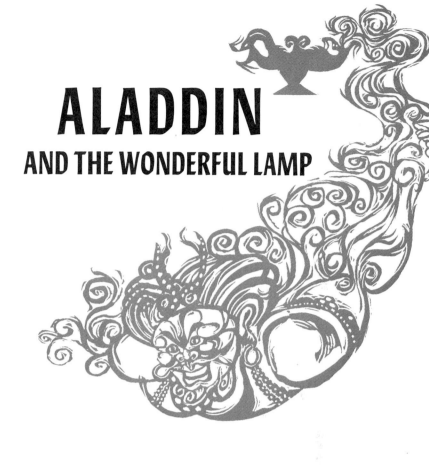

ALADDIN
AND THE WONDERFUL LAMP

Aladdin was the son of a poor tailor in one of the rich cities of China. His father died while Aladdin was yet very young, and his mother had to spin cotton day and night in order to support herself and him.

One day when he was about fifteen years old, he was playing in the streets with some of his companions. A stranger who was passing by stopped to look at him. This stranger was an African magician who was in need of the help of some young person. He knew at once that Aladdin was the boy who would be able to help him.

The magician first asked Aladdin's name of some persons standing near by. Then he went up to him and said, "My lad, are you not the son of Mustapha, the tailor?"

"Yes, sir," answered the boy, "but my father has been dead a long time."

At these words the magician threw his arms about Aladdin's neck, and with tears in his eyes, he said, "I am your uncle. Your father was my own brother. I knew you at first sight; you are so like him."

Then he gave Aladdin two pieces of gold, saying, "Go, my son, to your mother, and tell her that I will sup with her tonight."

Pleased with the money, Aladdin ran to his mother.

"Mother," said he, "have I an uncle?"

"No, child," replied his mother. "Your father had no brother, nor have I."

"I am just now come," said Aladdin, "from a man who says he is my father's brother. He gave me money and said that he would sup with you tonight."

The good woman was much surprised, but went out and bought food, and spent the day in preparing a supper. Just as the meal was ready, the magician knocked at the door, and came in loaded with all sorts of fruits and sweetmeats. He saluted Aladdin's mother, and with tears in his eyes, asked to be shown the place where his brother used to sit. As soon as they sat down to supper, he began to tell of his travels.

"My good sister," said he, "do not be surprised that you have never seen me before. I have been forty years away from this country, and during that time I have traveled in many lands. I am indeed sad to learn of my brother's death, but it is a comfort to find that he has so fine a son."

Then turning to Aladdin, he asked, "What business do you follow? Are you of any trade?"

Aladdin hung his head, and had nothing to say.

His mother replied, "Aladdin has never learned a trade. He does nothing but idle away his time in the streets."

"That is not well, Nephew," said the magician. "You must think of some way of earning a living. I will be glad to help you. If you like, I will take a shop for you and furnish it with fine linens."

Aladdin was full of joy at the idea. He told the magician that no business would please him better.

"Well, then," said the magician, "I will take you with me tomorrow, and clothe you as handsomely as any merchant in the city. Then we will open a shop."

He came again the next day, as he had promised, and took Aladdin to a merchant who sold all sorts of clothes. Aladdin chose those he liked best and put them on. The magician then took the boy to visit the finest shops in the city, and in the evening he gave him a feast.

When Aladdin's mother saw him return so well dressed, and heard him tell all that had happened, she was much pleased.

"Kind brother," said she to the magician, "I do not know how to thank you for all your goodness."

"Aladdin," he replied, "is a good boy, and well deserves all that I can do for him. I shall be very proud of him some day. Tomorrow I want to take him to see the gardens outside the town, and then the next day we will open the shop."

Aladdin rose very early the next morning, and ran to meet his uncle when he saw him coming. The magician led the boy out at one of the gates of the city to some beautiful gardens. They walked on and on, talking as they went, until they had gone far into the country.

When they grew tired, they sat down by a fountain of clear water, and the magician took from his girdle a box filled with cakes and fruits.

When they had eaten, they walked farther into the country, until they came to a narrow valley, with mountains on all sides. This was the place that the magician had hoped to reach. He had brought Aladdin here for a secret purpose.

"We will go no farther now," he said to the boy. "I will show you here some strange things that no one besides yourself will ever see. While I strike a light, gather up all the loose dry sticks you can see, to kindle a fire with."

Aladdin had soon gathered a great pile. The magician set fire to the wood, and when the flames arose, he threw in some incense. He then spoke two magic words, which Aladdin did not understand.

At once the earth opened at their feet. They could see a great stone with a brass ring fixed in it. Aladdin was so frightened that he would have run away, but the magician held him.

"If you will obey me," he said, "you will not be sorry. Under this stone there is hidden a treasure which will make you richer than all the kings in the world. But you must do exactly what I say."

Aladdin's fear was now gone, and he said, "Well, Uncle, what is to be done? I am ready to obey."

"Take hold of the ring," said the magician, "and lift up that stone."

Aladdin did as the magician told him, raised the stone and laid it on one side. When the stone was pulled up, there appeared a staircase three or four feet deep, leading to a door.

"Go down those steps," said the magician, "and open that door. It will lead you into a palace, divided into three great halls. In each of these you will see four vases full of gold and silver, but do not meddle with them. You must pass through the three halls without stopping. Above all, be very careful not to go near the outer walls, or even to touch them with your robe, for if you do so, you will die instantly.

"At the end of the third hall, you will find a door, which opens into a garden full of beautiful trees loaded with fruit. Walk across the garden to a wall, where you will see a niche before you, and in that niche a lighted lamp. Take the lamp down and put it out. Then throw away the wick and oil, and bring me the lamp."

After these words, the magician drew a ring from his finger, and put it on one of Aladdin's, saying, "This will protect you against all evil, so long as you obey me. Go now, my son; do as I have told you, and we shall both be rich all our lives."

Aladdin went down the steps, and opened the door. He found the three halls, just as the magician had said. He went through them carefully, and crossed the garden without stopping. He took the lamp from the niche, threw away the wick and the oil, and put the lamp in his girdle.

As he started back, he stopped in the garden to look at the fruit. The trees were loaded with fruits of different colors. Some were white, and others sparkled like crystals. Some were red and some green; some were blue, and others were violet. The white fruits were pearls; the sparkling ones were diamonds. The red ones were rubies; the green, emeralds, the blue, turquoises; and the purple, amethysts.

Aladdin did not know their value, and thought they were only glass. But the beautiful colors pleased him, and he gathered some of each kind. He filled both his pockets and his leather bag, too.

Loaded with the treasure, he hurried through the halls, and soon arrived at the mouth of the cavern. He saw the magician waiting for him, and called out,

"Give me your hand, Uncle, and help me out."

"First, give me the lamp," said the magician, "so that it may not hinder you."

"Indeed, Uncle," replied the lad, "I cannot now, but I will as soon as I am out."

The magician was determined that he would have the lamp before he would help the boy up. But Aladdin was so burdened with the fruit of the trees that he could not well get at the lamp.

The magician then flew into a rage, threw a little incense upon the fire, and spoke two magic words. At once the stone returned to its own place, and closed up the entrance of the strange cavern.

When Aladdin found himself in darkness, he called to the magician, telling him a thousand times that he would give him the lamp, but his cries were useless. He went to the bottom of the steps, thinking to enter the garden again, but the door was now shut.

For two days Aladdin remained in darkness without eating or drinking. At last he clasped his hands in prayer, and in so doing, he rubbed the ring which the magician had put upon his finger.

At once an enormous and frightful genie rose out of the earth, saying, "What do you wish? I am the slave of the ring, and will obey you in all things."

Aladdin replied, "Take me from this place."

At once the earth opened, and he found himself outside. He went home, but fell fainting at the door. When he came to himself, he told his mother what had passed, and showed her the lamp and the fruits he had gathered. He then asked for some food.

"Alas, child," she said, "I have nothing in the house, but I have spun a little cotton, and will go and sell it."

"Keep the cotton, Mother," said Aladdin, "and sell the lamp instead."

She took the lamp and began to rub it, for it was very dusty.

Instantly a frightful genie appeared, and cried with a loud voice, "What will you have? I am the slave of the lamp, and will obey those who hold it."

Aladdin's mother was too frightened to speak, but Aladdin seized the lamp, and said boldly, "Fetch me something to eat." The genie vanished, and in a moment returned, bearing on his head a silver tray. On the tray were twelve silver dishes filled with the finest food. There were also two silver plates and two silver cups. He placed the tray upon the table and again vanished.

Aladdin and his mother sat down and ate in great delight. Never before had they tasted such delicious food. When they had eaten all that the genie had brought, they sold the silver dishes, one by one, and got more food. In this way they lived well for some time.

One day, as he was walking in the city, Aladdin heard an order of the Sultan, telling all persons to close their shops and go into their houses while the Princess, his daughter, passed on her way to the bath.

Aladdin hid himself behind a door where he might see the Princess as she passed. He had not long to wait before she came with a great crowd of her maids. As she drew near the door where Aladdin was hiding, she threw aside her veil, and he saw her face. She was so beautiful that he loved her at first sight.

When Aladdin told his mother of his love for the Princess, she laughed and said, "Alas! My son, what can you be thinking of? You must be mad to talk thus."

"I am not mad," said Aladdin, "but in my right senses. I am determined to ask the Princess in marriage from the Sultan. You must go before him today to win his favor."

"I!" cried his mother. "I go to the Sultan! You know very well that no one can go before the Sultan without a rich gift, and where shall I find one?"

"Ah," said Aladdin, "I have a secret to tell you. Those bits of glass which I got from the trees in the cavern are jewels of great value. I have looked at the precious stones in all the shops, and none are so large and beautiful as mine. The offer of them, I am sure, will win the favor of the Sultan."

Then Aladdin brought the stones from the chest where they had been hidden, and his mother placed them in a fine china dish. The beauty of their colors amazed the mother, and she was certain that the gift could not fail to please the Sultan. She folded the dish and the jewels in a fine linen cloth, and set out to the palace of the Sultan.

The crowd of those who had business at the court was very great. The doors were opened, and she went in with the others, and placed herself in front of the Sultan. He, however, took no notice of her. She went every day for a week, and stood in the same place.

At last he sent for her and asked what she wanted of him. Trembling, the good woman told him of Aladdin's wish. The Sultan heard her kindly, and then asked her what she had in the napkin. She unfolded the cloth, and laid before him the sparkling jewels.

What was the surprise of the Sultan when he saw those jewels! For a long time he gazed at them without speaking. Then he exclaimed, "How very rich! How very beautiful!"

The Sultan, however, had planned that his daughter should

marry one of his own officers, and so he said to Aladdin's mother, "Tell your son that he shall marry my daughter, if he will send to me forty golden basins filled with jewels like these. They must be brought to me by forty black slaves, each of whom shall be led by a white slave, all richly dressed. Tell him that I await his answer."

The mother of Aladdin bowed low, and went home, thinking that all was lost. She gave Aladdin the message, adding, "He may wait long enough for his answer."

Aladdin smiled, and when his mother had gone out, he took the lamp and rubbed it. The genie instantly appeared, and Aladdin bade him bring the present that the Sultan had asked.

The genie vanished, and soon returned with forty black slaves, each carrying upon his head a golden basin filled with pearls, diamonds, rubies, and emeralds. The forty black slaves and the forty white slaves filled the house and the garden behind.

Aladdin bade them set out to the palace, two and two, and asked his mother to follow and present his gift to the Sultan. The slaves were so richly dressed that everyone in the city crowded to see them and the basins of gold that they carried on their heads.

They entered the palace and knelt before the Sultan. Each of the black slaves placed his basin upon the carpet, and then they stood in a semicircle about the throne.

The astonishment of the Sultan at the sight of these riches cannot be told. After gazing at the shining heaps of jewels, he finally roused himself and said to Aladdin's mother,

"Go, my good woman, and tell your son that I am waiting with open arms to welcome him."

The happy woman lost no time in giving the message to Aladdin, bidding him make haste. But Aladdin first called the genie.

"I want a scented bath," said he, "a rich robe, a horse as splendid as the Sultan's, and twenty slaves to attend me; and besides, twenty thousand pieces of gold in twenty purses."

All was done at once. Aladdin in a rich robe mounted his horse, and passed through the streets. Ten slaves marched on either side of him, and each carried a purse of gold to scatter among the people.

When the Sultan saw the handsome young man, he came down from his throne to greet him, and led him into a hall, where a great feast was spread. He wished Aladdin to marry his daughter, but Aladdin said, "I must first build a palace fit for her."

As soon as he reached home, he called the genie, and said, "Build me a palace of the finest marble, set with precious stones. There must be stables and horses and grooms and slaves."

The next morning the genie appeared and carried Aladdin to the palace. It was far more beautiful than Aladdin had hoped. Indeed, the Sultan and all his household were filled with wonder.

The marriage of Aladdin and the Princess was held the same day amid great rejoicing. Aladdin had won the love of the people by his kindness, and he lived for a time in great happiness.

Far away in Africa the magician found out by his magic arts that Aladdin was very rich and much beloved, instead of being dead in the cave. Filled with rage, he set out for China.

As he passed through the city, he heard everyone talking of the wonderful palace. He knew that it had been raised by the genie of the lamp, and he determined to get the lamp at any cost.

He was told by the merchants that Aladdin had gone a-hunting, and would not return for three or four days.

The magician then bought a dozen copper lamps, and went to the palace crying, "New lamps for old!"

When he came under the window of the Princess, all the slaves laughed as they heard the cry.

"Come," said one, "let us see if the old man means what he says. There is an ugly old lamp on the shelf. We will ask him to give us a new one in its place."

Now this was the magic lamp, which Aladdin had left there when he went hunting. The Princess, not knowing its value, laughed, and bade the slave take it and make the exchange.

The magician gladly gave for it the best lamp that he had, and then hurried away to the forest. When night came, he called the genie of the lamp, and commanded that the palace, the Princess, and he himself be carried before day to the farthest corner of Africa.

The grief of the Sultan was terrible when he found that the palace and his daughter had disappeared. Soldiers were sent to find Aladdin, who was brought bound before the Sultan. He would have been beheaded, had not the people begged for his life.

"I will spare your life," said the Sultan, "for forty days. Within that time you must find my daughter, or you will lose your head."

Aladdin wandered about like a madman, asking everyone that he met what had become of his palace, but the people only

laughed at him. At last he stopped at a little brook to drink some water. He made a cup of his hands, and in so doing rubbed the magic ring, which he still wore upon his finger.

The genie of the ring appeared, and asked his will.

"O mighty genie," cried Aladdin, "bring back my palace."

"That is not in my power," said the genie. "You must ask the slave of the lamp. I am only the slave of the ring."

"Then," said Aladdin, "take me where the palace is."

Instantly he found himself in a strange country, standing beside his own palace. The Princess was even then walking in her room, weeping. As she looked out of the window, she saw Aladdin, and she was filled with joy. She called to him to come to her, and she told him all that had happened.

When Aladdin heard of the exchange of the lamps, he knew at once that the magician was the cause of all his sorrow.

"Tell me," he asked, "where is the old lamp now?"

"The tyrant carries it in his girdle," said the Princess, "and never parts with it, by day or by night."

They talked together, and laid a plan for getting back the lamp. Aladdin went into the city and bought a powder that would cause instant death. The Princess dressed herself in rich robes, and invited the magician to sup with her.

While they were at the table, she ordered a slave to bring two cups of wine which she had prepared. The magician, pleased by her kindness, gladly drank the wine she gave him, and at once fell dead.

Aladdin, who was hiding near by, seized the lamp and called the genie, bidding him to carry the palace back to China.

A few hours later, the Sultan, looking from his window, saw Aladdin's palace sparkling in the sun. He ordered a great feast to be made ready, and there was merrymaking for a whole week.

After this Aladdin and his wife lived in peace. When the Sultan died, Aladdin ascended the throne, and ruled for many years.

(From *The Arabian Nights*)

HOW SHE KEPT HER GEESE WARM

* * * * * * By Hope Newell * * * * * *

One cold winter night, the Little Old Woman was out in the barn putting her geese to bed. She gave them some corn and took off their little red coats. Then she brushed each little coat with a whisk-broom and carefully shook out the wrinkles.

As she was folding the coats in a neat pile, she thought:

"My poor geese must be very cold at night. I have my cozy fire and my feather bed. But they have not even a blanket to keep them warm."

After the geese had eaten their corn, they began to go to roost.

"Honk, honk!" said the big gander, and he hopped up on the roost.

"Honk, honk!" said the grey goose, and she hopped up on the roost.

"Honk, honk!" said all the other geese, and they hopped up on the roost.

Then the Little Old Woman closed the barn door and went into the house. When she went to bed, she lay awake worrying about the geese. After a while she said to herself:

"I cannot sleep a wink for thinking how cold the geese must be. I had better bring them in the house where it is warm."

So the Little Old Woman dressed herself and went out to the barn to fetch the geese. She shooed them off the roost and put on their little red coats. She picked up two geese, and tucking one under each arm, she carried them into the house.

Then she went out to the barn and picked up two more geese. She tucked one goose under each arm and carried them into the house.

When the Little Old Woman had brought all the geese into the house, she said to herself:

"Now I must get them ready for bed again."

She took off their little red coats and gave the geese some corn. Then she brushed each little coat with a whisk-broom and carefully shook out all the wrinkles.

As she was folding the coats in a neat pile, she thought:

"It was very clever of me to bring the geese into the house. Now they will be warm, and I shall be able to sleep."

Then the Little Old Woman undressed herself again and went to bed.

After the geese had eaten their corn, they began to roost.

"Honk, honk!" said the gander, and he hopped up on the foot of the Little Old Woman's bed.

"Honk, honk!" said the grey goose, and she hopped up on the foot of the Little Old Woman's bed.

"Honk, honk!" said all the other geese, and they tried to hop up on the foot of the Little Old Woman's bed.

But it was not a very big bed, and there was not enough room for all the geese to roost. They began to fight. They pushed and shoved each other. They hissed and squawked and flapped their wings.

All night long the geese pushed and shoved each other. All night long they hissed and squawked and flapped their wings.

They made so much noise that the Little Old Woman did not sleep a wink.

"This will never do," she said. "When they were in the barn, I did not sleep for thinking how cold they must be. When they are in the house, I cannot sleep because they make so much noise. Perhaps if I use my head, I shall know what to do."

The Little Old Woman tied a wet towel around her forehead. Then she sat down with her forefinger against her nose and shut her eyes.

She used her head and used her head, and after a while she knew what to do.

"I will move the roost into the house," she said. "The geese will have the cozy fire to keep them warm. Then I will move my bed out into the barn. My feather bed will keep me warm, and I will not be worrying about the geese. They will not keep me awake with their noise. I shall sleep very comfortably in the barn."

The Little Old Woman moved the roost into the house, and she moved her bed out into the barn.

When night came again, she brought the geese into the house. After she had fed them some corn, she took off their little red coats. Then they all hopped up on the roost, and the Little Old Woman went out to the barn to sleep.

Her feather bed kept her as warm as toast. She was not worried about the geese, because she knew that they were warm too. So she slept as sound as a top all night long.

(From *The Little Old Woman Who Used Her Head*)

TALES FROM OTHER LANDS

WHY THE KANGAROO HOPS ON TWO LEGS

Adapted from a tale told by the Aborigines of Australia

Long, long ago—in the time the Aborigines call the Dream-time—Bohra, the kangaroo, did not hop on two legs as he does today. Instead, he walked on four legs, like a dog. And he had four long, pointed teeth, just as dogs do.

One bright, starry night, as Bohra was nibbling on grass and tender leaves, he heard the sound of singing. Looking up, he saw the red glow of many campfires twinkling through the darkness. Filled with curiosity, Bohra crept closer. When he drew near, he saw that the fires were arranged in a circle. Within the circle of fires, men were dancing. Their dark bodies were decorated with red and white designs. Stuck to some of the painted designs were tufts of fuzzy down from birds such as Gooloo, the magpie. Women sat outside the circle of fires, singing in clear voices. As they sang, they clicked clapsticks together and thumped on rolled-up possum skins. The people were holding a corroboree, or sacred ceremony.

Round and round went the dancing men. Faster and faster went the *click-click-click* of the clapsticks. Louder and louder went the *thump-thumpah-thump* on the possum skins. The fires flickered in the darkness. Overhead, the stars sparkled and the Milky Way stretched across the sky like a bright, glowing river.

As Bohra watched, he grew more and more interested. The clicking and thumping excited him. The singing and dancing thrilled him. He felt that he, too, wanted to dance—just as the men were dancing. Suddenly, standing up on his hind legs so that he would look like the men, he jumped into the circle of fires! Balancing himself with his tail, he began to hop behind the dancers.

At the sight of him, the women stopped singing and began to shriek and point. The men stopped dancing and looked to see what the trouble was. When they saw Bohra standing on his hind legs trying to imitate them, some were angry. "Kill him!" they shouted. But others said, "No, no. Let us see him dance."

The women were told to start their singing again, to beat the possum skins and click their clapsticks. As they did so, the men began to dance. And after them, at the end of the line, came Bohra. He was hopping on two legs and trying to do what the men did.

As the men danced, they turned their heads to watch Bohra. Soon they began to grin and chuckle. Bohra looked very funny hopping around so seriously, a timid expression on his face, and his tail leaving a snakelike track behind him. Finally, the men were laughing so hard they had to stop dancing.

Then, one of the men had an idea. He led the others out of the circle and into the surrounding darkness. There he had them gather bundles of long grass. He told them what he wanted them to do, and the men quickly went to work.

After a time, the men called to the women to pile more wood on the fires and start their singing. As the fires rose higher and higher, the women clicked their clapsticks, thumped on the possum skins, and raised their voices in song. Then the line of painted men came back into the circle of fires. But now, hanging from the backs of their belts were long, crude tails of woven grass.

The men began to dance the way Bohra danced. They hopped round the ring as Bohra did, their grass tails waggling behind them. They held their arms up in front of them, with their hands dangling down, the way Bohra held his forepaws as he danced. The men looked so funny the women could hardly manage to sing.

At last, with a great "Hooh! Hooh! Hooh!" from the dancers, the singing and clicking and thumping faded into silence. The tired dancers sank to the ground. It was nearly dawn. Already the laughing cries of the kookaburra birds could be heard.

After a few moments, an old wirinun, or magician, stood up. "This Bohra came to our corroboree without being invited. He must be shown that he has no right to do this," said the wirinun. "But, we will not kill him, for he has shown us a new dance. Instead, from now on, he and all his tribe shall hop on their hind legs, using their tails to balance themselves—just as he hopped when he was dancing. And they shall hold their forepaws up in front of them, just as he did." Motioning to the others to follow him, he said, "Now, let us make this Bohra one of us. He and his tribe shall be our brothers. Then, if any of them see our corroborees, they will not tell others what they have seen."

The men took Bohra into the trees, away from the fires and the women. There they performed the ceremony that made him a member of their tribe. It was the same ceremony that their young boys went through when they came of age. As part of the ceremony, the wirinun took a boomerang and knocked out Bohra's long, pointed teeth.

From that day to this, no kangaroo has had these long, pointed teeth. And to this very day, every kangaroo hops on two legs, the way Bohra did that night when he joined the corroboree. And ever since that time, when the people of the Bohra tribe have a corroboree, they put on tails made of woven grass. Then they dance the kangaroo dance—just as Bohra danced it on that starry night in the long-ago Dreamtime.

GONE IS GONE

Retold by Wanda Gág

This is an old, old story which my grandmother told me when I was a little girl. When she was a little girl her grandfather had told it to her, and when he was a little peasant boy in Bohemia, his mother had told it to him. And where she heard it, I don't know, but you can see it is an old, old story, and here it is, the way my grandmother used to tell it.

It is called *Gone Is Gone* and it is the story of a man who wanted to do housework.

This man, his name was Fritzl—his wife, her name was Liesi. They had a little baby, Kinndli by name, and Spitz who was a dog.

They had one cow, two goats, three pigs, and of geese they had a dozen. That's what they had.

They lived on a patch of land, and that's where they worked.

Fritzl had to plow the ground, sow the seeds and hoe the weeds. He had to cut the hay and rake it too, and stack it up in bunches in the sun. The man worked hard, you see, from day to day.

Liesi had the house to clean, the soup to cook, the butter to churn, the barn yard and the baby to care for. She, too, worked hard each day as you can plainly see.

They both worked hard, but Fritzl always thought that he worked harder. Evenings when he came home from the field, he sat down, mopped his face with his big red handkerchief, and said: "Hu! How hot it was in the sun today, and how hard I did work. Little do you know, Liesi, what a man's work is like, little do you know! *Your* work now, 'tis nothing at all."

"'Tis none too easy," said Liesi.

"None too easy!" cried Fritzl. "All you do is to putter and potter around the house a bit—surely there's nothing hard about such things."

"Nay, if you think so," said Liesi, "we'll take it turn and turn about tomorrow. I will do your work, you can do mine. I will go out in the fields and cut the hay, you can stay here at home and putter and potter around. You wish to try it—yes?"

Fritzl thought he would like that well enough—to lie on the grass and keep an eye on his Kinndli-girl, to sit in the cool shade and churn, to fry a bit of sausage and cook a little soup. Ho! that would be easy! Yes, yes, he'd try it.

Well, Liesi lost no time the next morning. There she was at peep of day, striding out across the fields with a jug of water in her hand and the scythe over her shoulder.

And Fritzl, where was he? He was in the kitchen, frying a string of juicy sausages for his breakfast. There he sat, holding the pan over the fire, and as the sausage was sizzling and frizzling in the pan, Fritzl was lost in pleasant thoughts.

"A mug of cider now," that's what he was thinking. "A mug of apple cider with my sausage—that would be just the thing."

No sooner thought than done.

Fritzl set the pan on the edge of the fireplace, and went down into the cellar where there was a big barrel full of cider. He pulled the bung from the barrel and watched the cider spurt into his mug, sparkling and foaming so that it was a joy to see.

But Hulla! What was that noise up in the kitchen—such a scuffle and clatter! Could it be that Spitz-dog after the sausages? Yes, that's what it was, and when Fritzl reached the top of the stairs, there he was, that dog, dashing out of the kitchen door with the string of juicy sausages flying after him.

Fritzl made for him, crying, "Hulla! Hulla! Hey, hi, ho, hulla!" But the dog wouldn't stop. Fritzl ran, Spitz ran too. Fritzl ran fast, Spitz ran faster, and the end of it was that the dog got away and our Fritzl had to give up the chase.

"Na, na! What's gone is gone," said Fritzl, shrugging his shoulders. And so he turned back, puffing and panting, and mopping his face with his big red handkerchief.

But the cider, now! Had he put the bung back in the barrel? No, that he hadn't, for here he was still holding the bung in his fist.

With big fast steps Fritzl hurried home, but it was too late, for look! the cider had filled the mug and had run all over the cellar besides.

Fritzl looked at the cellar full of cider. Then he scratched his head and said, "Na, na! What's gone is gone."

Well, now it was high time to churn the butter. Fritzl filled the churn with good rich cream, took it under a tree and began to churn with all his might. His little Kinndli was out there too, playing Moo-cow among the daisies. The sky was blue, the sun right gay and golden, and the flowers, they were like angels' eyes blinking in the grass.

"This is pleasant now," thought Fritzl, as he churned away. "At last I can rest my weary legs. But wait! What about the cow? I've forgotten all about her and she hasn't had a drop of water all morning, poor thing."

With big fast steps Fritzl ran to the barn, carrying a bucket of cool fresh water for the cow. And high time it was, I can tell you, for the poor creature's tongue was hanging out of her mouth with the long thirst that was in her. She was hungry too, as a man could well see by the looks of her, so Fritzl took her from the barn and started off with her to the green grassy meadow.

But wait! There was that Kinndli to think of—she would surely get into trouble if he went out to the meadow. No, better not take the cow to the meadow at all. Better keep her nearby on the roof. The roof? Yes, the roof! Fritzl's house was not covered with shingles or tin or tile—it was covered with moss and sod, and a fine crop of grass and flowers grew there.

To take the cow up on the roof was not so hard as you might think, either. Fritzl's house was built into the side of a hill. Up the little hill, over a little shed, and from there to the green grassy roof. That was all there was to do and it was soon done.

The cow liked it right well up there on the roof and was soon munching away with a will, so Fritzl hurried back to his churning.

But Hulla! Hui! What did he see there under the tree?

Kinndli was climbing up on the churn—the churn was tipping! spilling! falling! and now, there on the grass lay Kinndli, all covered with half-churned cream and butter.

"So that's the end of our butter," said Fritzl, and blinked and blinked his blue eyes. Then he shrugged his shoulders and said, "Na, na! What's gone is gone."

He picked up his dripping Kinndli and set her in the sun to dry. But the sun, now! It had climbed high up into the heavens. Noontime it was, no dinner made, and Liesi would soon be home for a bite to eat.

With big fast steps Fritzl hurried off to the garden. He gathered potatoes and onions, carrots and cabbages, beets and beans, turnips, parsley and celery.

"A little of everything, that will make a good soup," said Fritzl as he went back to the house, his arms so full of vegetables that he could not even close the garden gate behind him.

He sat on a bench in the kitchen and began cutting and paring away. How the man did work, and how the peelings and parings did fly!

But now there was a great noise above him. Fritzl jumped to his feet.

"That cow," he said, "she's sliding around right much up there on the roof. She might slip off and break her neck."

Up on the roof went Fritzl once more, this time with loops of heavy rope. Now listen carefully, and I will tell you what he did with it. He took one end of the rope and tied it around the cow's middle. The other end of the rope he dropped down the chimney and this he pulled through the fireplace in the kitchen below.

And then? And then he took the end of the rope which was hanging out of the fireplace and tied it around his own middle with a good tight knot. That's what he did.

"Oh yo! Oh ho!" he chuckled. "That will keep the cow from falling off the roof." And he began to whistle as he went on with his work.

He heaped some sticks on the fireplace and set a big kettle of water over it.

"Na, na!" he said. "Things are going as they should at last, and we'll soon have a good big soup! Now I'll put the vegetables in the kettle—"

And that he did.

"And now I'll put in the bacon—"

And that he did too.

"And now I'll light the fire—"

But that he never did, for just then, with a bump and a thump, the cow slipped over the edge of the roof after all; and Fritzl— well, he was whisked up into the chimney and there he dangled, poor man, and couldn't get up and couldn't get down.

Before long, there came Liesi

home from the fields with the water jug in her hand and the scythe over her shoulder.

But Hulla! Hui! What was that hanging over the edge of the roof? The cow? Yes, the cow, and half-choked she was, too, with her eyes bulging and her tongue hanging out.

Liesi lost no time. She took her scythe—and ritsch! rotsch!—the rope was cut, and there was the cow wobbling on her four legs, but alive and well, heaven be praised!

Now Liesi saw the garden with its gate wide open. There were the pigs and the goats and all the geese too. They were full to bursting, but the garden, alas! was empty.

Liesi walked on, and now what did she see? The churn up-turned, and Kinndli there in the sun, stiff and sticky with dried cream and butter.

Liesi hurried on. There was Spitz-dog on the grass. He was full of sausages and looked none too well.

Liesi looked at the cellar. There was the cider all over the floor and halfway up the stairs besides.

Liesi looked in the kitchen. The floor! It was piled high with peelings and parings, and littered with dishes and pans.

At last Liesi saw the fireplace. Hu! Hulla! Hui! What was that in the soup-kettle? Two arms were waving, two legs were kicking, and a gurgle, bubbly and weak-like, was coming up out of the water.

"Na, na! What can this mean?" cried Liesi. She did not know (but we do—yes?) that when she saved the cow outside, something happened to Fritzl inside. Yes, yes, as soon as the cow's rope was cut, Fritzl, poor man, he dropped down the chimney and crash! splash! fell right into the kettle of soup in the fireplace.

Liesi lost no time. She pulled at the two arms and tugged at the two legs—and there, dripping and spluttering, with a

218

cabbage-leaf in his hair, celery in his pocket, and a sprig of parsley over one ear, was her Fritzl.

"Na, na, my man!" said Liesi. "Is that the way you keep house —yes?"

"Oh Liesi, Liesi!" sputtered Fritzl. "You're right—that work of yours, 'tis none too easy."

"'Tis a little hard at first," said Liesi, "but tomorrow, maybe, you'll do better."

"Nay, nay!" cried Fritzl. "What's gone is gone, and so is my housework from this day on. Please, please, my Liesi—let me go back to my work in the fields, and never more will I say that my work is harder than yours."

"Well then," said Liesi, "if that's how it is, we surely can live in peace and happiness for ever and ever."

And that they did.

(From *Gone Is Gone*)

THE **FIVE** CHINESE BROTHERS

Once upon a time there were Five Chinese Brothers and they all looked exactly alike. They lived with their mother in a little house not far from the sea.

The First Chinese Brother could swallow the sea.

The Second Chinese Brother had an iron neck.

The Third Chinese Brother could stretch and stretch and stretch his legs.

The Fourth Chinese Brother could not be burned.

And the Fifth Chinese Brother could hold his breath indefinitely.

Every morning the First Chinese Brother would go fishing, and whatever the weather, he would come back to the village with beautiful and rare fish which he had caught and could sell at the market for a very good price.

By Claire Huchet Bishop and Kurt Wiese

One day, as he was leaving the market place, a little boy stopped him and asked him if he could go fishing with him.

"No, it could not be done," said the First Chinese Brother.

But the little boy begged and begged and finally the First Chinese Brother consented. "Under one condition," said he, "and that is that you shall obey me promptly."

"Yes, yes," the little boy promised.

Early next morning, the First Chinese Brother and the little boy went down to the beach.

"Remember," said the First Chinese Brother, "you must obey me promptly. When I make a sign for you to come back, you must come at once."

"Yes, yes," the little boy promised.

Then the First Chinese Brother swallowed the sea.

And all the fish were left high and dry at the bottom of the sea. And all the treasures of the sea lay uncovered.

The little boy was delighted. He ran here and there stuffing his pockets with strange pebbles, extraordinary shells and fantastic algae.

Near the shore the First Chinese Brother gathered some fish while he kept holding the sea in his mouth. Presently he grew tired. It is very hard to hold the sea. So he made a sign with his hand for the little boy to come back. The little boy saw him but paid no attention.

The First Chinese Brother made great movements with his arms and that meant "Come back!" But did the little boy care? Not a bit and he ran further away.

Then the First Chinese Brother felt the sea swelling inside him and he made desperate gestures to call the little boy back. But the little boy made faces at him and fled as fast as he could.

The First Chinese Brother held the sea until he thought he was going to burst. All of a sudden the sea forced its way out of his mouth, went back to its bed . . . and the little boy disappeared.

When the First Chinese Brother returned to the village,

alone, he was arrested, put in prison, tried and condemned to have his head cut off.

On the morning of the execution he said to the judge:

"Your Honor, will you allow me to go and bid my mother good-bye?"

"It is only fair," said the judge.

So the First Chinese Brother went home . . . and the Second Chinese Brother came back in his place.

All the people were assembled on the village square to witness the execution. The executioner took his sword and struck a mighty blow.

But the Second Chinese Brother got up and smiled. He was the one with the iron neck and they simply could not cut his head off. Everybody was angry and they decided that he should be drowned.

On the morning of the execution, the Second Chinese Brother said to the judge:

"Your Honor, will you allow me to go and bid my mother good-bye?"

"It is only fair," said the judge.

So the Second Chinese Brother went home . . . and the Third Chinese Brother came back in his place.

He was pushed on a boat which made for the open sea.

When they were far out on the ocean, the Third Chinese Brother was thrown overboard.

But he began to stretch and stretch and stretch his legs, way down to the bottom of the sea, and all the time his smiling face was bobbing up and down on the crest of the waves. He simply could not be drowned.

Everybody was very angry, and they all decided that he should be burned.

On the morning of the execution, the Third Chinese Brother said to the judge:

"Your Honor, will you allow me to go and bid my mother good-bye?"

"It is only fair," said the judge.

So the Third Chinese Brother went home . . . and the Fourth Chinese Brother came back in his place.

He was tied up to a stake. Fire was set to it and all the people stood around watching it. In the midst of the flames they heard him say:

"This is quite pleasant."

"Bring some more wood!" the people cried.

The fire roared higher.

"Now it is quite comfortable," said the Fourth Chinese Brother, for he was the one who could not be burned. Everybody was getting more and more angry every minute and they all decided to smother him.

On the morning of the execution, the Fourth Chinese Brother said to the judge:

"Your Honor, will you allow me to go and bid my mother good-bye?"

"It is only fair," said the judge.

So the Fourth Chinese Brother went home . . . and the Fifth Chinese Brother came back in his place. A large brick oven had been built on the village square and it had been all stuffed with whipped cream. The Fifth Chinese Brother was shovelled into the oven, right in the middle of the cream, the door was shut tight, and everybody sat around and waited.

They were not going to be tricked again! So they stayed there all night and even a little after dawn, just to make sure.

Then they opened the door and pulled him out. And he shook himself and said, "My! That was a good sleep!"

Everybody stared open-mouthed and round-eyed. But the judge stepped forward and said, "We have tried to get rid of you in every possible way and somehow it cannot be done. It must be that you are innocent."

"Yes, yes," shouted all the people. So they let him go and he went home.

And the Five Chinese Brothers and their mother all lived together happily for many years.

(From *The Five Chinese Brothers*)

THE OLD MAN WITH THE BUMP

Long, long ago, there lived an old man who had a large bump on his right cheek. It grew larger and larger each day, and he could do nothing to make it go away.

"Oh, dear, how will I ever rid myself of this bump on my cheek," sighed the old man; and though he went from doctor to doctor throughout the countryside, not one of them could help him.

"You have been a good and honest man," said his wife. "Surely some day there will be someone who can help you."

And so, the old man kept hoping each day that this "someone" would come along soon.

Retold by Yoshiko Uchida

Now one day the old man went out into the hills to collect
some faggots for his fire. When the sun began to dip behind the
hills, he strapped a large bundle of wood on his back and slowly
began the long walk back to his little house at the foot of the
hill. Suddenly the sky began to darken, and soon huge drops of
rain splashed down on the wooded hillside. The old man hur-
riedly looked about for some shelter, and before long spied a
gnarled old pine tree with a large hollow in its trunk.

"Ah, that will be a good shelter for me during the storm," he said to himself, and he quickly crawled into the hollow of the tree. He did this just in time too, for soon the rain poured down from the skies as though someone had overturned an immense barrel of water up in the heavens. The old man crouched low as the thunder crashed above his head and the lightning made weird streaks of light in the dark forest.

"My, what a storm this is!" he said to himself, and closed his eyes tight. But it was just a thundershower, and it stopped as suddenly as it had begun. Soon, all the old man could hear was the drip, drop . . . drop . . . of the rain slipping down from the shiny pine needles.

"Ah, now that the rain has stopped I must hurry home, or my wife will worry about me," said the old man.

He was about to crawl out of the hollow of the tree, when he heard a rustling like the sound of many, many people walking through the forest.

"Well, there must have been other men caught in the forest by the storm," he thought, and he waited to walk home with them. But suddenly the old man turned pale as he saw who was making the sounds he had heard. He turned with a leap, and jumped right back into the hollow of the tree. For the footsteps weren't made by men at all. They were made by many, many ghosts and spirits walking straight toward the old man.

The old man was so frightened he wanted to cry out for help, but he knew no one could help him.

"Oh, dear, ohhhh, dear," moaned the old man, as he buried his head in his hands. "What will they do to me?"

But soon he raised his head ever so slightly, for he thought he heard music in the air. Yes, there were singing voices and laughing voices floating toward him. The old man lifted his head a little more and ever so carefully took a peek to see what they were doing. His mouth fell wide open in surprise at the sight before his eyes. The spirits were gaily dancing about on the soft carpet of pine needles. They laughed and sang as they whirled and twirled about. They were feasting, and drinking, and making merry.

"A feast of spirits! My, I have never seen such a strange sight," said the old man to himself. Soon he forgot to be afraid and he poked his head further and further from the hollow of the tree. The old man's feet began to tap in time to the music, and he clapped his hands along with the spirits. His head swayed from side to side and he smiled happily as he watched the strange sight before him.

Now he could hear the leader saying, "Such foolish dances! I want to see some really fine dancing. Is there no one here who can do any better?"

Before he knew what he was doing, the old man had jumped right out of the hole, and danced out among the ghosts.

"Here, I will show you something different! I will show you some fine dancing," he called. The spirits stepped back in surprise and the old man began to dance before them. With so many spirits watching him, the old man did his very best, and danced as he had never danced before.

"Good, very good indeed," said the leader of the spirits, nodding his head in time to the music.

"Yes, yes," agreed the others. "We have never seen such fine dancing!"

When the old man stopped, the spirits crowded about him, offering him food and drink from their feast.

"Thank you, thank you," said the old man happily. He breathed a sigh of relief as he saw that he had pleased the spirits, for he had feared that they might harm a mortal such as he.

The leader of the spirits then stepped before the old man and said in a deep, low voice, "We would like to see more of such fine dancing. Will you return again tomorrow, old man?"

"Yes, yes, of course I will come," answered the old man, but the other spirits shook their ghostly heads and lifted warning fingers.

"Perhaps this mortal will not keep his word," they protested. "Let us take a forfeit from him—something which he treasures most—then he will be sure to return for it tomorrow."

"Ah, a fine plan indeed," answered the leader. "What shall we take from him?"

All the spirits stepped around the old man, and examined him from head to toe to see what would make a good forfeit.

"Shall it be his cap?" asked one.

"Or his jacket?" asked another.

Then finally one spoke up in a loud and happy voice, "The bump on his cheek! The bump on his cheek! Take that from him and he will be sure to come for it tomorrow, for I have heard that such bumps bring good luck to human beings, and that they treasure them greatly."

"Then that shall be the forfeit we will take," said the leader, and with one flick of his ghostly finger he snatched away the bump on the old man's cheek. Before he could say Oh the spirits had all disappeared into the dusky woods.

The old man was so surprised he scarcely knew what to do. He looked at the spot where the spirits had just been standing and then rubbed the smooth, flat cheek where once the bump had been.

"My goodness! My, my," murmured the old man. Then with a big smile on his face he turned and hurried home.

Now the old woman had been very worried, for she was afraid that the old man had met with an accident during the storm. She stood in the doorway of their cottage waiting for him to return, and when at last she saw him trudging down the road, she hastened to greet him.

"My, but I was worried about you," she said. "Did you get drenched in that thundershower?" Then suddenly the old woman stopped talking and looked carefully at the old man.

"Why, wh-hy, where is the bump on your right cheek? Surely you had it this morning when you went out into the woods!"

The old man laughed happily and told the old woman all

about his meeting with the spirits. "So you see, I have lost my bump at last!" he added.

"My, isn't that nice!" exclaimed the old woman, admiring the old man's right cheek. "We must celebrate this happy occasion," she said, and together they feasted with *akano gohan* and *tai*.

Early the next morning they heard a knock on their door, and there stood the greedy man who lived next door to them. He had come to borrow some food, as he so often did.

Now this man also had a bump on his cheek, but his was on the left side of his face. When he saw the old man without his bump, he threw up his hands in surprise and exclaimed, "Why, what has happened? Where is the bump on your face?" He peered closely at the old man's face and said, "How I would like to get rid of mine too! Perhaps I can if I do exactly as you did." Then, because he wanted the same good fortune, he asked anxiously, "Tell me, exactly what did you do?"

So the old man carefully explained how he hid in the hollow of an old tree until the spirits came to dance in the dusk. Then he told about the dance he did for them and how they took his bump for a forfeit.

"Ah, thank you, my friend," said the neighbor. "Tonight I shall do exactly the same thing." And after borrowing a large sack of the old man's rice, he hurried home.

That evening, the greedy neighbor trudged out into the woods and found the same tree. He slipped into the hollow trunk and waited quietly, peeking out every once in a while to watch for the spirits. Just as the sky began to darken and the setting sun painted all the clouds in gold, the spirits again twirled and whirled out into the small clearing in front of the old tree.

The leader looked about and said, "I wonder if the old man who danced for us yesterday will soon be here?"

"Yes, yes. Here I am!" called the greedy neighbor, as he leaped from the hollow tree trunk. He opened out a fan and then he began his dance. But alas and alack, this old man had never learned how to dance. He hopped from one foot to the other, and shook his head from side to side, but the spirits were not smiling as they had been the day before. Instead they scowled and frowned, and called out, "This is terrible. We have no use for you, old man. Here, take back your precious bump," and with a big THUMP the leader flung the bump on the greedy man's right cheek. Then the spirits disappeared into the woods just as quickly as they had come.

"Ohhhhh!" cried the greedy man as he sadly walked home. "Never again will I try to be someone else."

Now he not only had a big bump on his left cheek, he had one on his right cheek too. And so the greedy man who had tried to copy his neighbor went home looking just like a chipmunk with both cheeks full of nuts!

(From *The Dancing Kettle and Other Japanese Folk Tales*)

WHY THE BEAR HAS A STUMPY TAIL

Retold by George Webbe Dasent

One winter's day the Bear met the Fox, who came slinking along with a string of fish he had stolen.

"Hi, stop a minute! Where did you get those fish?" demanded the Bear.

"Oh, my Lord Bruin, I've been out fishing and caught them," said the Fox. So the Bear had a mind to learn to fish, too, and bade the Fox tell him how he was to set about it.

"Oh, it is quite easy," answered the Fox, "and soon learned. You've only got to go upon the ice, and cut a hole and stick your tail down through it, and hold it there as long as you can. You're not to mind if it smarts a little; that's when the fish bite. The longer you hold it there, the more fish you'll get, and then all at once out with it, with a cross pull sideways and a strong pull, too."

Well, the Bear did as the Fox said, and though he felt very cold, and his tail smarted very much, he kept it a long, long time down in the hole, till at last it was frozen in, though of course he did not know that. Then he pulled it out with a strong pull, and it snapped short off, and that's why Bruin goes about with a stumpy tail to this day!

(Old Norse Folk Tale)

the SKUNK

in TANTE ODETTE'S OVEN

Retold by Natalie Savage Carlson

Once in another time, my friends, an old woman called Tante Odette lived in Canada. She was a plump little woman with beady, black eyes, a pouf of a moustache and a double chin. She lived at the edge of the village in a neat whitewashed house with a sharp roof and two dormer windows.

Tante Odette was all alone except for the beasts in the barn and Chouchou, the big gray cat who lived in the house with her.

She worked her own little field and cared for her beasts all by herself because she was too stingy to pay anyone to help her.

For this reason, things did not always go so smoothly for her. The ox broke through the fence or the well froze over or the roof began leaking.

There was that Tuesday morning that she got up very early to start the fire in her outdoor oven. The fat loaves were rising nicely in the pans, the weather was pleasant and there was plenty of dry wood for the fire. It looked like a day in which everything would go right from beginning to end.

Tante Odette gathered a load of wood in her arms and carried it over to the oven. She laid it down in a neat pile and picked up a stick. She noticed that the oven door had been left open, so she poked her stick inside to see that no leaves or twigs had blown in. The stick would not go in very far because something was in the way.

The old woman stooped lower and peered into the dark depths of the oven. The sight that met her eyes caused her to scream and slam the door shut.

She went running out of her yard and down the road as fast as her bunions and old bones would take her.

At Albe Roberge's farm, she saw Albe drawing water from the well.

"Albe, Albe," she cried breathlessly, "come quick! There is a skunk in my oven."

Albe let the bucket sink back into the well. He stared at Tante Odette in astonishment.

"Are you sure it is a skunk?" he asked. "Perhaps it is your cat."

"Believe me," said Tante Odette, "if that skunk had turned his weapon on me, you would not have to ask such a question. Of course it is a skunk. Is my Chouchou a black cat with a white stripe down his back?"

Then as Albe still stood there as stupidly as François Ecrette's simple son, René, she explained the whole matter to him.

"I went out early to start the fire in my oven," she began. "I carried a load of wood in my arms, like this. I laid it down, over here. I picked up this stick, see. The oven door was open so I poke, poked the stick inside, but something was in the way. It was a skunk. A skunk is in my oven."

At last Albe Roberge seemed to understand.

"I will come right over as soon as I draw a bucket of water," he promised.

Tante Odette turned and hurried back to the road. But she did not go home. She headed for the farm of Jean Labadie. If two heads were better than one, three would be even more dependable.

Jean Labadie was on his way to his henhouse with a pail of chicken feed in his hand. Tante Odette panted up to him.

"Jean, Jean Labadie," she cried. "Come quickly! There is a skunk in my oven."

Jean Labadie regarded her politely.

"Are you sure it is a skunk?" he asked. "Perhaps it is a scrap of old fur coat that you threw away."

Tante Odette was becoming quite exasperated with her neighbors. When faced by an emergency, they seemed even more simple-minded than René Ecrette, who went slap, slapping through the fields, talking to the birds and bushes.

"Of course it is a skunk," she insisted. "Would I throw away a scrap of anything? Am I such a spendthrift?"

Jean had to agree that she was anything but a spendthrift.

"I went out early to start the fire for my baking," she went on. "I carried a load of wood in my arms, like this. I laid it down, over here. I picked up this stick, see. The oven door was open so I poke, poked the stick inside. But something was in the way. It was a skunk—in my oven."

Tante Odette moaned and wrung her plump hands.

"I will come over as soon as I have fed the chickens," promised Jean Labadie.

Then the old woman turned and limped toward André Drouillard's farm. The wits of her neighbors seemed unusually dull on this fresh morning that had turned sour so unexpectedly. She would need all the heads she would like to knock together.

André Drouillard was just coming out of his back door. He looked surprised to see Tante Odette calling at such an hour, for the old woman was not given to neighborliness.

"André Drouillard," she wheezed, "come quickly. There is a skunk in my oven."

"Are you sure it is a skunk?" blinked André. "Perhaps you saw a shadow inside as you opened the door."

Tante Odette was outraged.

"Does a shadow have a bushy tail?" she demanded. "Does it have two shiny black eyes? Does it grit its teeth at me? No! It was this way. I went out early to start the fire in my oven. I carried a load of wood in my arms, like this. I laid it down, over here. I picked up this stick, see. The oven door was open so I poke, poked my stick inside, but something was in the way. It was a skunk."

André's face brightened.

"Why didn't you tell me that at first?" he asked. "I will come right over."

So as long as her breath came and went, Tante Odette stumbled from farm to farm seeking help. And everyone came quickly, for although a skunk in one's oven is a calamity, a skunk in the oven of one's neighbor is an interesting diversion. Not since the past Sunday had so many people traveled down the dusty road.

Albe Roberge and his family were the first to arrive, Jean Labadie came on their heels. Albe opened the oven door, peered in, then carefully closed it.

"It is a skunk indeed," he said.

Then Jean Labadie opened the door, peered in also, then closed it just as carefully.

"Yes, you are right," he admitted. "It *is* a skunk."

In pairs and threes and fours, the people of the parish arrived. There were five of the blue-eyed Meloches, making jokes with pretty Eulalie Beneteau to make her dimples wink. Henri Dupuis, the storekeeper, who looked as if he had just eaten one of the pickles out of his own crock, was only two skips behind his gossipy wife, Hortense. There were Delphine Langlois, the old maid, and several others who did not matter and would certainly be of no help.

And each one must look in the oven for himself, close the door

and name the uninvited occupant a skunk.

Since everyone who wanted to help had arrived and no one denied that a skunk was in Tante Odette's oven, it was now time to think of some way to get the skunk out.

"I will run home and get my gun," cried Jean Labadie. "I'll put a quick end to that caller."

"No, no," howled Tante Odette, "not in my oven."

"Not in the oven," agreed all the others. "She would not be able to bake bread in it for a month—perhaps never."

"And it would spoil the pelt," added Albe Roberge, who trapped for the trader and knew what he was talking about.

"Perhaps we should get somebody's dog," suggested one of the blue-eyed Meloches. "A dog would bark and frighten him out of the oven."

"No, no," cried Tante Odette, "the skunk must not be frightened while he is in my oven."

Everyone agreed that this was true. A frightened skunk was apt to be a very unpleasant fellow.

"Perhaps we should tie a piece of meat on a string and coax him out," said someone else. "Get a piece of meat, Tante Odette."

"I have no meat," snapped the old woman, "and I wouldn't waste it on a skunk if I had."

So this plan was dropped because no one else cared to use his meat to coax a skunk out of Tante Odette's oven.

"Someone should get the priest," suggested Madame Roberge. "He might know what to do." But the others thought that it was more a matter for Dr. Brisson.

"He could give him a pill that would put him to sleep," said one, "then we could carry the skunk out into the woods."

"No, no," cried Albe Roberge, "do not let such a fine pelt get away. I will take care of the skunk once he is asleep."

Then the youngest Meloche howled with laughter.

"Ha, ha!" he roared, "and that will be one surprised skunk when he wakes up and finds his skin on Albe Roberge's board and Dr. Brisson's bill in his bare paw."

Then everybody but Tante Odette laughed and a light mood fell upon the crowd. André Drouillard was reminded of the time he had worked in the lumber camps and a porcupine had gotten caught in his boot one night.

"And believe me, my friends," he added, "a porcupine wedged in a boot makes as big a problem as a skunk in an oven."

That promptly set Jean Labadie off on a long tale about a deer that was accidentally shut up in the barn with his cows one winter.

"And when spring came, that doe had twin fawns that I raised with my own calves," he ended.

If old Gabriel Meloche had been there with his fiddle and Tante Odette's bread already baked, the whole thing could have been a gay fete.

Only Tante Odette could not forget the reason that everyone had dropped his work at the start of the morning to hurry to her little farm.

"The skunk!" she reminded them. "The skunk is still in my oven. How can I bake bread today?"

One by one, the neighbors walked over to the oven, opened the door, looked surprised to see the skunk still there, then carefully closed the door again.

"Yes," said each one in turn, "he is still there."

And while this was going on, Samigish the Indian came riding down the road on his sway-backed pony. When he saw all the people in Tante Odette's yard, waiting with the air of those about to sit down to a feast, he dismounted and made his way through the gate.

Tante Odette was overjoyed to see an Indian entering her yard. After all this was more of a problem for one close to nature.

"Samigish," she cried, "come help us. There is a skunk in my oven. We need your help."

"You sure him skunk?" asked Samigish, who had never heard of a skunk in a white man's oven. Bread or venison or a ham, yes, but never a skunk.

"Of course it's a skunk," said Albe Roberge with disgust, for by this time everyone could see what a foolish question this made.

Samigish opened the door, looked in, then carefully closed the door again.

"What shall we do?" asked Tante Odette.

243

Samigish licked his lips.

"Young, tender skunk," he said. "Anybody got match?"

"Oh, no, no," screamed Tante Odette, "not in my oven."

Everyone tried at once to explain to the Indian that the skunk was not to be cooked.

Samigish stared at them in puzzlement. He shrugged his shoulders.

"Then why skunk in oven?" he asked.

But he did not wait for an answer. Answers never really explained the white man's queer ways. He mounted his sway-backed pony and rode away without another word.

By now, all the people were becoming a little bored with the skunk matter, and it did not look as if Tante Odette was going to serve any food or drink.

Jean Labadie remembered that he hadn't milked his cow.

André Drouillard spoke of the job of cleaning his barn.

Madame Roberge said it was long past time for breakfast.

It was at this stage that René Ecrette, the simple son of François, came slap, slapping his feet down the road with his head bobbling about like a loose cork. His dull eyes brightened at sight of the gathering in Tante Odette's yard. Like Samigish, he thought that where there was a crowd of people, there must be food. He turned in.

At the time René entered the yard, Tante Odette was quite at the end of her wits. She made one desperate attempt to do something about the skunk in the oven. This René might be simple-minded, it was true, but it was said that he talked to the birds and the trees. Perhaps he had a way with wild things.

The old woman went running to him, twisting the folds of her apron.

"René," she cried, "René Ecrette. There is a skunk in my oven. Can you get him out without frightening him?"

René nodded his head gravely. And he didn't ask "Are you sure it is a skunk?"

"Then do something," implored Tante Odette.

René nodded again.

"What will you do?" asked Tante Odette.

But René did not answer her. He slap, slapped over to the

oven and opened the door. He leaned inside. The people could hear him talking in a low, earnest voice. No one could hear what he said because his head was inside the oven. And no one cared to venture closer to try to hear. There was a tight feeling in the air, and Tante Odette felt it from the knot on top of her head to the bunions on her feet.

At last René stepped back. Everyone stared and stretched his neck. For a few moments nothing happened. Then the sharp face of the skunk appeared in the doorway of the oven. Everyone stepped back a few feet. The skunk clumsily wriggled over the edge and dropped to the ground.

Slowly he started through the yard. The crowd respectfully parted to make a wide path for him—a very, very wide path.

The skunk marched toward the woods. He walked with majesty, his flag of truce held high, and not even Albe Roberge, the trapper, blocked his way. In awe, all watched him disappear into the bushes.

Tante Odette was delighted. The others were amazed. They gathered around René Ecrette.

"How did you get him to come out?" asked André Drouillard.

"What did you say to him?" asked Jean Labadie.

René Ecrette hung his head and swung his arms back and forth because he was not used to such admiring attention from the people of the parish. At last he was persuaded to tell the secret.

"I just told him that if he stayed in the oven any longer," he said, "he would begin to smell like Tante Odette's bread, and none of the other skunks would come near him."

So you see, my friends, only the simple-minded René Ecrette was wise enough to know that even a skunk, the lowliest of beasts, has his self-respect and values the good opinion of his own kind.

(From *The Talking Cat and Other Stories of French Canada*)

WHO WAS ANANSI?

He was a man and he was a spider.

When things went well he was a man, but when he was in great danger he became a spider, safe in his web high up on the ceiling. That was why his friend Mouse called him "Ceiling Thomas."

Anansi's home was in the villages and forests of West Africa. From there long years ago thousands of men and women came to the islands of the Caribbean. They brought with them the stories that they loved, the stories about clever Br'er Anansi, and his friends Tiger and Crow and Moos-Moos and Kisander the cat.

Today the people of the islands still tell these stories to each other. So, in some country village in Jamaica when the sun goes down the children gather round an old woman and listen to the stories of Anansi.

In the dim light they see the animals—Goat, Rat, Crow, and the others—behaving like men and women. They see how excited everyone becomes as soon as Anansi appears. They laugh at the way in which he tricks all the strong animals and gets the better of those who are much bigger than himself. At last the story comes to an end. The night and bedtime come. But next day when the children see Ceiling Thomas they know that he is more than a spider. They know that he is Anansi, the spider man, and they do him no harm.

ANANSI
AND THE PLANTAINS

By Philip M. Sherlock

It was market day, but Anansi had no money. He sat at the door of his cottage and watched Tiger and Kisander the cat, Dog and Goat, and a host of others hurrying to the market to buy and sell. He had nothing to sell, for he had not done any work in his field. Turtle had won the few coins that he had saved in the broken calabash that he kept hidden under his bed. How was he to find food for his wife Crooky and for the children? Above all, how was he to find food for himself?

Soon Crooky came to the door and spoke to him. "You must go out now, Anansi, and find something for us to eat. We have nothing for lunch, nothing for dinner, and tomorrow is Sunday. What are we going to do without a scrap of food in the house?"

"I am going out to work for some food," said Anansi. "Do not worry. Every day you have seen me go with nothing and come home with something. You watch and see!"

Anansi walked about until noon and found nothing, so he lay down to sleep under the shade of a large mango tree. There he slept and waited until the sun began to go down. Then, in the cool of the evening, he set off for home. He walked slowly, for he was ashamed to be going home empty-handed. He was asking himself what he was to do, and where he would find food for the children, when he came face to face with his old friend Rat going home with a large bunch of plantains on his head. The bunch was so big and heavy that Brother Rat had to bend down almost to the earth to carry it.

Anansi's eyes shone when he saw the plantains, and he stopped to speak to his friend Rat.

"How are you, my friend Rat? I haven't seen you for a very long time."

"Oh, I am staggering along, staggering along," said Rat. "And how are you—and the family?"

Anansi put on his longest face, so long that his chin almost touched his toes. He groaned and shook his head. "Ah, Brother Rat," he said, "times are hard, times are very hard. I can hardly find a thing to eat from one day to the next." At this tears came into his eyes, and he went on:

"I walked all yesterday. I have been walking all today and I haven't found a yam or a plantain." He glanced for a moment at the large bunch of plantains. "Ah, Br'er Rat, the children will have nothing but water for supper tonight."

"I am sorry to hear that," said Rat, "very sorry indeed. I know how I would feel if I had to go home to my wife and children without any food."

"Without even a plantain," said Anansi, and again he looked for a moment at the plantains.

Br'er Rat looked at the bunch of plantains, too. He put it on the ground and looked at it in silence.

Anansi said nothing, but he moved toward the plantains. They drew him like a magnet. He could not take his eyes away

from them, except for an occasional quick glance at Rat's face. Rat said nothing. Anansi said nothing. They both looked at the plantains.

Then at last Anansi spoke. "My friend," he said, "what a lovely bunch of plantains! Where did you get it in these hard times?"

"It's all that I had left in my field, Anansi. This bunch must last until the peas are ready, and they are not ready yet."

"But they will be ready soon," said Anansi, "they will be ready soon. Brother Rat, give me one or two of the plantains. The children have eaten nothing, and they have only water for supper."

"All right, Anansi," said Rat. "Just wait a minute."

Rat counted all the plantains carefully and then said, "Well, perhaps, Br'er Anansi, perhaps!" Then he counted them again and finally he broke off the four smallest plantains and gave them to Anansi.

"Thank you," said Anansi, "thank you, my good friend. But, Rat, it's four plantains; and there are five of us in the family—my wife, the three children, and myself."

Rat took no notice of this. He only said, "Help me to put this bunch of plantains on my head, Br'er Anansi, and do not try to break off any more."

So Anansi had to help Rat to put the bunch of plantains back on his head. Rat went off, walking slowly because of the weight of the bunch. Then Anansi set off for his home. He could walk quickly because the four plantains were not a heavy burden. When he got to his home he handed the four plantains to Crooky, his wife, and told her to roast them. He went outside and sat down in the shade of the mango tree until Crooky called out to say that the plantains were ready.

Anansi went back inside. There were the four plantains, nicely roasted. He took up one and gave it to the girl. He gave one each to the two boys. He gave the last and biggest plantain to his wife. After that he sat down empty-handed and very, very sad-looking, and his wife said to him, "Don't you want some of the plantains?"

"No," said Anansi, with a deep sigh. "There are only enough for four of us. I'm hungry, too, because I haven't had anything to eat; but there are just enough for you."

The little child asked, "Aren't you hungry, Papa?"

"Yes, my child, I am hungry, but you are too little. You cannot find food for yourselves. It's better for me to remain hungry as long as your stomachs are filled."

"No, Papa," shouted the children, "you must have half of my plantain." They all broke their plantains in two, and each one gave Anansi a half. When Crooky saw what was happening she gave Anansi half of her plantain, too. So, in the end, Anansi got more than anyone, just as usual.

(From *Anansi, the Spider Man*)

THE BIRDS THAT COULD NOT BE SEEN

Adapted from a Polynesian legend

Far out in the deep Pacific Ocean lie the beautiful islands of Polynesia where people today still tell stories about Maui. They say he was part man and part god, born long ago with eight heads, and tossed into the sea by his mother who thought he was dead. They say the sea god saved Maui, who later lost seven of his heads. The head that remained was so full of tricks and magic that sometimes Maui angered the gods, and made people wonder what he would do next.

Before he brought the gift of fire to warm the people and to cook their food, they say he set the world on fire. They say he pushed up the sky so that people could stand instead of crawl. They say he lassoed the sun god and beat him with a club, forcing him to move more slowly across the sky so that people could have more time to plant and harvest.

They say he caught a giant fish at the bottom of the ocean, changed it into the islands of Tonga, Rakahanga, Hawaii, and the North Island of New Zealand, and placed them where they are today.

They say Maui did these things and a thousand more when he was fully grown, yet even as a boy, he played a magical trick that people still tell about.

On the island where Maui came to live with his mother and four older brothers, people could hear chirps and whistles. They could also hear the flutter of wings. But, they never saw any birds. Indeed, they did not even know such creatures lived.

Once, Maui's brothers asked, "Mother, who whistles and chirps as the sun comes up? Who fans the air and touches our cheeks so softly when we play in the forest?"

Their mother answered, "Perhaps the gods are pleased with my children, so they make pleasant sounds and caress you."

Maui grinned at his mother's answer, but said nothing. Of all the people on the island, Maui was the only one who could see and hear the birds. They were his only real friends, and for him they sang their sweetest songs.

One stormy day at sea, the winds swept ashore an outrigger canoe. It came from a faraway land. Aboard was a man who looked down his nose at the people, their clothes, and their houses. He even turned up his nose at their food.

"How unfortunate I was to be forced ashore on this miserable island," he complained. "In my country, the earth is greener. The sky is bluer. The people are better looking, and they are richer. We have fine houses and better food. How can you people live in such a dreadful place?"

He talked on and on about all the wonders to be found in his country. He made the people feel ashamed. They had nothing grand to show their guest; nothing that would please him or make them proud of their land.

Maui listened to the man until he could stand it no longer. He sped into the forest and called to the birds.

"My friends," he said, "I need your help to make the people as happy as they were before the stranger arrived on this island."

"We will do whatever you wish," said the birds.

"Then follow me," said Maui. "When I clap my hands, sing as you have never sung before."

The birds lifted their wings with a great flutter and, flying overhead, followed Maui to the place where the people sat listening with lowered heads to the stranger.

Maui clapped his hands, making a sound as loud as thunder. At once, the birds began to sing in a chorus of thousands. The music was so unexpected, so thrilling, and so beautiful that the stranger stopped talking for the first time since his arrival. Even the people were surprised. Never before had they heard such melodies. They raised their heads and began to smile.

When the birds became silent, the stranger said, "I can see nothing around here that could possibly make such sounds. I have traveled in many lands but never have I heard anything to compare with what I've just heard. How proud I would be if I could say that such sounds could be heard in my country. Where did that wonderful music come from?"

Before anyone could answer, Maui leaped to the center of the gathering. He was determined that never again would the people be ashamed of their land. He raised his arms toward the sky and in a loud, clear voice that echoed for miles, he began to chant a magic command that only the birds understood.

Suddenly, all around them, the people saw feathered creatures flying and twirling, spinning and soaring, looping and dipping. They saw the creatures perched on every branch of every tree and on the thatched roof of every house—birds of colors as brilliant as the golden sun and the jeweled sea. Never had the people seen such color—red birds and yellow birds, blue birds and green birds, pink birds and purple birds. Everybody saw every bird there was to see on the island. Each bird warbled or whistled, chirped or chittered, singing as it flew, filling the air with music and color.

The people looked in awe at the birds, and then they looked in awe at Maui. Now they knew that he was more than a boy who liked to play tricks. He was surely part god. They whispered, "What a wonderful thing it is that Maui is one of us. If he can make such magic now, what will he do when he's fully grown?"

In the years that followed, Maui's many magical deeds gave them their answer.

HALVAR'S HOUSE

Adapted from a Swedish folk tale

High in the hills of Sweden stands a big, empty house made of strangely shaped stones. People in the neighborhood call it the children's playhouse, the favorite playing place of children for more years than anyone now living can recall. How did the house get there?

Some people say that long ago the stone house belonged to a giant named Halvar, a most unusual giant—the only poor giant that ever lived. Halvar was poor because he was always giving things away. This made him happy, and everyone who knew him loved him.

On sunny days, Halvar sat on a huge rock outside his front door and talked to people on their way to town in the valley.

One day, Halvar saw a stranger approaching, leading a cow. What a cow! The poor thing was nothing but skin and bones, and its owner did not look much better. Indeed, Halvar could not remember when he had seen a sorrier looking pair.

The stranger smiled at Halvar. "Good morning, sir," he said pleasantly. "Can you tell me if I am on the right road to the town in the valley?"

"You are," replied Halvar. "Are you going to market to sell your cow?"

"Yes," said the stranger. "My wife and I bought a small farm. The cow came with it. You can see for yourself what an old bag of bones the cow is. Perhaps I can trade her for some flour.

"Things have been going so badly, my wife and I have not eaten a good meal for months. Our chickens don't lay eggs. The weeds in the field grow faster than I can cut them. They choke the wheat so that there is hardly enough to make flour to bake a loaf of bread.

"But I'd better be going to market while the crowds are still there. Maybe I'll have a better chance to trade this good-for-nothing beast." The farmer tipped his straw hat, and started on his way.

"Wait a moment," said Halvar. "How would you like to trade your cow for seven fat goats?"

The farmer could hardly believe his ears. "You don't look any richer than I," he said. "Why on earth should you want to give me seven fat goats for one skinny cow?"

"I like you," said Halvar, "and I want to help you. Leave the cow in your barn and tomorrow morning you will find seven fat goats in her place."

The farmer was suspicious. He had never known such generosity. But the cow was more trouble than she was worth, so the farmer decided to take a chance.

The farmer went home and put the cow in the barn. He stayed awake most of the night, tossing and turning.

"What a fool I was to listen to the giant," he said to himself. "When morning comes, the cow will be gone, the barn will be empty, and I will be poorer than ever."

At dawn, he arose, quickly dressed, and rushed to the barn.

259

He pulled open the barn door. Yes, the cow was gone. But in her place stood seven of the finest, fattest goats the farmer had ever seen.

From that day on, the farmer's luck began to change. The goats gave so much milk there was plenty to drink and enough left over to make into cheese. The farmer sold the cheese at the market, and used the money to buy chickens. The chickens laid more than enough eggs for the farmer and his wife to eat, so they sold the extra eggs at the market and bought fine new clothes. Best of all, the goats ate the weeds in the field so that the wheat grew strong and tall. There was more than enough wheat to make all the flour the farmer's wife needed to bake as many loaves of bread as she wanted. The farmer sold the bread at the market and bought new furniture. In time, the farmer and his wife became so rich that they forgot about once having been poor. And they forgot about poor Halvar, the giant.

One day, the farmer was on his way to attend a meeting with the mayor of the town. The farmer was a very important man now. Again he chanced to be passing Halvar's door. This time the farmer was riding a beautiful, golden-brown horse.

"My friend," Halvar called out, "don't you remember me? Stop and join me for some lunch. I would like to talk to you."

The farmer was impatient to be on his way. "Of course, I remember you. I just haven't the time to spare," he said angrily. "I have far more important things to do than to spend time with those who do nothing but sit in the sun all day. I'll give you some advice. If you have too much to eat, keep the leftovers for another day. Then maybe you'll be as rich and important as I am. Now, good day to you."

Halvar watched the farmer and his horse gallop out of sight. The sun was shining but Halvar felt so gloomy that he went into the house and closed the door.

Suddenly, Halvar smiled. "I don't know why I should feel sad just because some people don't know how to accept good fortune," he thought. "It makes me happy to help people and I shall go on giving things away until I have nothing left to give." And he went outside, and sat in the sun, and talked to the people, and was as friendly and happy as ever.

Perhaps that is why the house he once lived in, high in the hills of Sweden, is forever filled with good cheer and happiness. And perhaps that is why, down through the years, children have found Halvar's house a fine place to play.

THE CLEVER FROG

Adapted from an African folk tale

In a village in Africa there once lived a young man named Nzua, who wished to marry the beautiful daughter of Lord Sun and Lady Moon. So Nzua wrote a letter asking for permission to marry Lord Sun's daughter. But how could Nzua send the letter to Lord Sun who lived in a house in the sky?

Nzua went into the forest where he saw a deer. "Mbambi," he said, "will you take my letter to Lord Sun?"

The deer replied, "I would like to help you, but no matter how high I leap, I cannot leap as high as the sky."

Nzua waited until he saw a hawk. "Kikuambi," he said, "will you take my letter to Lord Sun?"

"Don't be silly," replied the hawk. "No one can fly that high."

Soon Nzua saw a holokoko bird. "Holokoko," he said, "surely, you will take my letter to Lord Sun."

The holokoko bird replied, "I can fly higher than all other birds, but even so, I cannot fly as high as the house of Lord Sun."

Nzua went home and sat down to think how he might send his letter to Lord Sun. He thought until his head ached. Suddenly, something cold touched his big toe. He looked down. There sat Frog.

"Young master," said Frog, "give me your letter. I will take it to Lord Sun."

Nzua frowned. "Go away, Frog. I have asked Mbambi, Kikuambi, and Holokoko. The deer can leap, and the birds fly high. Yet, they cannot reach the sky. How then can you, a little green hopping creature, do what they cannot do?"

"Give me the letter," said Frog, "and you will see."

"All right," said Nzua, "but if you fail, I shall beat you."

Now, Frog knew that Lord Sun and his family drank water that came from a certain well in the village. Each morning Frog saw Lord Sun's servant girl climb down a cobweb ladder to the well with an empty water jug on her shoulder. She would lower the jug into the well. When the jug filled with water, she would pull it up, and carry it back to Lord Sun's house.

Frog held the letter in his mouth and jumped into the well. As soon as the servant girl lowered the jug, Frog hopped into it and was carried to Lord Sun's house. The servant girl placed the jug on a table in the room where the water was kept. Frog heard the door close. He hopped out of the jug and put the letter on the table. Then he hid in a corner, and waited.

In a little while, Lord Sun came into the room. He saw the letter and read it. He called the servant girl. "Did you bring this letter from Nzua?" he asked.

"Master," said the servant girl, "I did not bring the letter. I do not even know this Nzua."

Lord Sun was puzzled. He put the letter into his pocket and went away.

The next morning, Frog hopped into the empty water jug and was carried back to the well where Nzua was waiting. "Well," said Nzua, "did you bring an answer?"

"Young master," replied Frog, "Lord Sun read your letter but he gave no answer."

"I do not believe you went to Lord Sun's house," Nzua shouted, raising his hand to beat Frog.

"Do not beat me," begged Frog. "Please give me another chance! Write another letter, and when Lord Sun reads it, he will surely answer it this time."

Nzua glared at Frog. "I don't know whether I can trust you," he said angrily. He thought for a few minutes while Frog hopped up and down nervously. At last Nzua said, "All right, I'll give you one more chance."

"Thank you, master," said Frog.

Just as before, Frog went to Lord Sun's house, put the second letter on the table, and hid in a corner.

Lord Sun was more puzzled than ever when he saw the second letter. He wrinkled his forehead and tugged at his ear. He looked around the room and under the table and out the window. Frog held his breath and kept out of sight. Finally Lord Sun said, "I do

not see anyone. I wonder who brought this letter?" Again he called to the servant girl. "Did you bring this letter?" he asked.

Again the servant girl replied, "Master, I did not bring this letter. Truly, I do not know this Nzua."

Lord Sun shook his head. "This man Nzua must have magical powers," he said. "How else could the letters get here? He must be an important man, also. Otherwise, why would he have such powers?" He sat at the table. "Bring me paper and pen. I will answer this letter."

Lord Sun wrote, "To you who sends letters asking to marry my daughter, I will agree. But first you must send me a sackful of pure gold to prove that you are able to care for my daughter."

When Frog brought the letter to Nzua, Nzua said, "Oh Frog, what will I do now? How will I get enough pure gold to fill a sack?"

"Do not worry," said Frog. "I will help you. Go home and get a shovel. Then I will take you to a place deep in the forest where you will find enough pure gold to fill a sack. Also bring food. You

will need strength, for it will take much walking and hard work."

Nzua did as Frog told him. Three days and three nights they walked until they reached the place deep in the forest. Three more days and three more nights Nzua shoveled and shoveled and shoveled. Finally, the shovel struck something hard—a large, round, clay pot. "What is this?" asked Nzua, tired and disappointed.

"Lift the lid and see," said Frog.

Nzua lifted the lid and saw enough pure gold to fill a sack.

Then Frog took the sackful of gold to Lord Sun's house and put it on the table, and hid in a corner.

Lord Sun's eyes glowed when he saw the gold. He sat down and wrote another letter at once. "Nzua, by your magical powers, and the gift of gold, you have proved that you love my daughter and will be able to care for her. You may marry her in my house in the sky." He placed the letter on the table and left the room.

"Frog," Nzua said after reading the letter, "you have done what no one else could do, and I thank you. But all is in vain. How can I go to the house in the sky? I am too big to hide in a water jug, and too heavy to climb the cobweb ladder."

"Don't worry," said Frog, "I will think of a way so that you can marry the princess."

The next morning, Frog took his magic kalubungu box with him to Lord Sun's house. He hopped out of the jug and hid under the princess's bed where he stayed until the princess was fast asleep. Then, without waking her, he took her voice from her and put it in his magic kalubungu box. Someone was coming, so Frog hid again under the princess's bed. He heard Lord Sun say, "Lady Moon, what is the matter with the princess? She opens her mouth, but no sound comes. What shall we do?"

Frog returned to earth the next morning. He gave Nzua the kalubungu box containing the voice of the princess. "Young master," Frog said, "write another letter to Lord Sun. Tell him that you have the magic to restore his daughter's voice, if he sends the princess to you on earth."

After Lord Sun read this letter, he said, "Put on your bride's dress, daughter, and go to Nzua. He has the magic to make you well. He will be a good husband."

And so it was that Frog helped Nzua's wish come true.

I have told my little story. It is finished.

The Poppy Seed Cakes

By Margery Clark

Once upon a time there was a little boy and his name was Andrewshek. His mother and his father brought him from the old country when he was a tiny baby.

Andrewshek had an Auntie Katushka and she came from the old country, too, on Andrewshek's fourth birthday.

Andrewshek's Auntie Katushka came on a large boat. She brought with her a huge bag filled with presents for Andrewshek and his father and his mother. In the huge bag were a fine feather bed and a bright shawl and five pounds of poppy seeds.

The fine feather bed was made from the feathers of her old green goose at home. It was to keep Andrewshek warm when he took a nap.

The bright shawl was for Andrewshek's Auntie Katushka to wear when she went to market.

The five pounds of poppy seeds were to sprinkle on little cakes which Andrewshek's Auntie Katushka made every Saturday for Andrewshek.

One lovely Saturday morning Andrewshek's Auntie Katushka took some butter and some sugar and some flour and some milk and seven eggs and she rolled out some nice little cakes. Then she sprinkled each cake with some of the poppy seeds which she had brought from the old country.

While the nice little cakes were baking, she spread out the fine feather bed on top of the big bed, for Andrewshek to take his nap. Andrewshek did not like to take a nap.

Andrewshek loved to bounce up and down and up and down on his fine feather bed.

Andrewshek's Auntie Katushka took the nice little cakes out of the oven and put them on the table to cool; then she put on her bright shawl to go to market. "Andrewshek," she said, "please watch these cakes while you rest on your fine feather bed. Be sure that the kitten and the dog do not go near them."

"Yes, indeed! I will watch the nice little cakes," said Andrewshek. "And I will be sure that the kitten and the dog do not touch them." But all Andrewshek really did was to bounce up and down and up and down on the fine feather bed.

"Andrewshek!" said Andrewshek's Auntie Katushka, "how can you watch the poppy seed cakes when all you do is to bounce up and down and up and down on the fine feather bed?" Then Andrewshek's Auntie Katushka, in her bright shawl, hurried off to market.

But Andrewshek kept bouncing up and down and up and down on the fine feather bed and paid no attention to the little cakes sprinkled with poppy seeds.

Just as Andrewshek was bouncing up in the air for the ninth time, he heard a queer noise that sounded like "Hs-s-s-s-sss," at the front door of his house.

"Oh, what a queer noise!" cried Andrewshek. He jumped down off the fine feather bed and opened the front door. There stood a great green goose as big as Andrewshek himself. The goose was very cross and was scolding as fast as he could. He was wagging his head and was opening and closing his long red beak.

"What do you want?" said Andrewshek. "What are you scolding about?"

"I want all the goose feathers from your fine feather bed," quacked the big green goose. "They are mine."

"They are not yours," said Andrewshek. "My Auntie Katushka brought them with her from the old country in a huge bag."

"They are mine," quacked the big green goose. He waddled over to the fine feather bed and tugged at it with his long red beak.

"Stop, Green Goose!" said Andrewshek, "and I will give you one of Auntie Katushka's poppy seed cakes."

"A poppy seed cake!" the green goose quacked in delight. "I love nice little poppy seed cakes! Give me one and you shall have your feather bed."

But one poppy seed cake could not satisfy the greedy green goose.

"Give me another!" Andrewshek gave the green goose another poppy seed cake.

"Give me another!" the big green goose hissed and frightened Andrewshek nearly out of his wits.

Andrewshek gave him another and another and another till all the poppy seed cakes were gone.

Just as the last poppy seed cake disappeared down the long neck of the green goose, Andrewshek's Auntie Katushka appeared at the door, in her bright shawl. "Boo! hoo!" cried Andrewshek. "See! that naughty green goose has eaten all the poppy seed cakes."

"What? All my nice little poppy seed cakes?" cried Andrewshek's Auntie Katushka. "The naughty goose!"

The greedy goose tugged at the fine feather bed again with his long red beak and started to drag it to the door. Andrewshek's Auntie Katushka ran after the green goose and just then there was a dreadful explosion. The greedy goose who had stuffed himself with poppy seed cakes had burst and his feathers flew all over the room.

"Well! well!" said Andrewshek's Auntie Katushka, as she gathered up the pieces of the big green goose. "We soon shall have two fine feather pillows for your fine feather bed."

(From The Poppy Seed Cakes)

270

MYTHS AND LEGENDS

The Touch
of Midas

Adapted from a Greek Legend

Once there was a king named Midas who lived in a shiny palace and had almost everything a human being could want—a good wife, a beautiful blonde daughter, a green-eyed cat, dishes of silver and gold, and a palace full of servants to wait on him and his family.

Yet Midas was grumpy. His single pleasure was hoarding gold, and he couldn't seem to get enough of it. He liked gold so much that he even named his daughter Marygold. He hid the gold pieces he had in wooden chests in his room. He spent many hours each day counting his gold. And just before bedtime, he'd open the chests one more time just to look at the gold and touch it.

One day, as he was hovering over his gold, a quivering shadow appeared beside him. Midas was sure it was a visit from one of the gods. Suddenly, the shadow spoke. "I am a messenger of the gods. I come to grant you anything you want—but mind you, just one thing."

"Oh," cried the king without hesitating, "I want everything that I touch to be turned into gold!"

"Your wish is granted," the shadow said and faded away.

At that moment, Midas turned back to his wooden chests and ran his hand over the top of one of them. Instantly, the wood turned into gold. Midas' eyes widened with disbelief. He ran to his favorite chair and touched it, and just like that—gold. He sat down excitedly in his new golden chair. It wasn't as comfortable as it used to be, because the soft downy pillow turned to cold hard gold, too.

"No matter," thought Midas, "I can stand a little discomfort for a solid gold chair."

Before dinner, he took a walk in his garden to try his new gift on some of the flowers. He touched a poppy. It turned to gold, stem and all. Midas giggled with delight. Then he touched a rose and a daisy. Instantly, they turned into gold, too. He managed to work up quite an appetite while turning a dozen or more flowers into gold.

His servants had prepared a beautiful table for the king, with roast lamb, hot broth and bread, and a bowl piled high with fresh fruit.

"What a miraculous and wonderful thing has happened to me," thought Midas as he picked up his broth to sip it. The instant he touched the bowl, it turned into gold. So did the broth inside. He reached for the lamb, for he was very hungry. It, too, turned into gold. Poor Midas! Whatever was he to do? He then grabbed the bread with one hand and an apple with the other. They both turned into lumps of gold in his hands.

"I'll starve," cried the king. He was beginning to think his golden touch wasn't as wonderful as he first thought it was.

With a long sad face, he slumped in his golden chair, thinking about the fate that was in store for him. Just then, the cat jumped onto the king's lap. Without thinking, the king stroked the soft fur. The cat's back arched, its fur bristled. On the spot, the cat turned into gold. And the bristles turned into sharp golden needles. I'll surely ruin my entire kingdom if I'm not stopped, thought Midas. While he was deep in his thoughts, Marygold ran into the room looking for the cat. When she saw the golden cat standing like a statue, she cried. Midas ached

with sympathy for his beloved daughter and went to her to offer her comfort. As he touched her shoulder, she froze gold. Midas was horrified.

"Lock me up! Put me away!" he cried, "before I touch another thing."

The gods had been watching Midas. They heard his plea and felt sorry for him. The quivering shadow appeared once again at his side and spoke: "King Midas, if you wish to rid yourself of your golden touch. . . ."

Midas interrupted and pleaded, "Anything, I'll do anything."

"Go to the river," the voice instructed, "and wash your hands in the water. Then return to the palace with a pail of the water and sprinkle it over all that you have touched."

Midas picked up his robes and ran toward the river. He stopped short at the edge of the garden. Yipes, the pail! He ran back, grabbed a pail, and began again his race to the river—tripping, panting, falling once—but running as fast as his legs would carry him.

He reached the river bank, fell to his knees, and plunged his hands in and out of the water, rubbing and wringing them together. Then he filled the pail with water and returned in haste to the place where he had left Marygold. He dipped his hand into the pail and flicked his wet fingers toward her. As the sprinkles of water hit her, she revived and started to move. Her golden skin returned to its rosy hue. But she was crying and puzzled over the cat, just as she had been before she turned to gold. Midas fixed that. He sprinkled the cat with a few drops of water. In an instant the cat was alive again.

Midas told Marygold about his golden touch and took her to the garden to show her the flowers. Then he sprinkled them back to flowers again.

By this time, his stomach was growling for food. He had forgotten how long it had been since he had eaten. He looked toward the table, and there were the golden lumps of food he had left some hours before. He could scarcely believe that his fondness for gold now had turned to disgust. He changed the food back to food again and ate. And no one has ever enjoyed a dinner more than King Midas did that night.

From that time forward, Midas spent most of his time cultivating his garden. And the lowliest weed gave him more pleasure than a hundred pieces of gold.

Pandora

Adapted from Nathaniel Hawthorne

Long, long ago, when this old world was very young, there lived a boy named Epimetheus. He had neither father nor mother, and so that he might not be lonely, a little girl—who like himself had no father or mother—was sent from a far country to live with him and be his playmate. Her name was Pandora.

The first thing that Pandora saw, when she entered the cottage where Epimetheus lived, was a great box. And almost the first question which she asked was:

"Epimetheus, what's in that box?"

"That's a secret," answered Epimetheus, "and you must be kind enough not to ask any questions about it. The box was left here to be kept safely. Even I don't know what's in it."

"But who gave it to you?" asked Pandora, "and where did it come from?"

"That is a secret, too," answered Epimetheus.

"Ridiculous!" exclaimed Pandora, pouting her lip. "I wish the great ugly box were out of the way!"

"Just don't think about it any more," snapped Epimetheus. "Let's go outside and play."

They ran out to play, and for a while Pandora forgot all about the box. But when she came back to the cottage, she couldn't help thinking about it again.

"Where did that box come from?" she kept saying to herself and to Epimetheus. "And what in the world can be inside?"

"I've told you fifty times, I don't know what's inside," said Epimetheus.

"You might open it," Pandora persisted, "and then we could see for ourselves."

"Pandora, what are you thinking of!" exclaimed Epimetheus. He was shocked at the idea of opening a box that had been given to him to take care of.

"At least," said she, "you can tell me how it came here."

"It was left at the door," replied Epimetheus, "just before you came, by a person who was dressed in an odd kind of cloak. He had a cap that seemed to be made partly of feathers, so that it looked as if it had wings."

"Oh, I know him," said Pandora. "It was Quicksilver, and he brought me here, as well as the box. No doubt he intended it for me, and probably it contains pretty dresses for me to wear, or toys for you and me to play with, or something very nice for us both to eat!"

"Perhaps so," answered Epimetheus, turning away, "but until Quicksilver comes back and tells us we may, neither of us has any right to lift the lid of the box," and he went out of the cottage.

"What a stupid boy he is!" muttered Pandora.

Then she stood gazing at the box. It was made of a beautiful dark wood, so highly polished that Pandora could see her face in it.

The most beautiful face was carved in the center of the lid. Pandora had looked at this face a great many times, and it seemed to her that, at times, it smiled at her and, at other times, it had a grave look that rather frightened her.

The box did not have a lock and key, as most boxes have, but it was tied with a gold cord.

Pandora said to herself, "Perhaps if I untied the cord, I could tie it up again. There would be no harm in that. I need not open the box, even if the knot is untied."

Just then, by accident, she gave the knot a little twist, and the gold cord untwined itself, as if by magic, and there was the box, without any fastening.

"Oh, dear," said Pandora. "What will Epimetheus say when

he finds the knot untied? He will know that I have done it. How shall I make him believe that I have not looked into the box?"

And then the thought came into her head that, since he would think she had looked into the box, anyway, she might just as well have a little peep.

The face on the lid smiled at her, as if to say there could be no harm in raising the lid. And then she thought she could hear tiny voices inside the box that whispered,

"Let us out, dear Pandora—pray, let us out! We will be such nice pretty playmates for you!"

"What can it be?" thought Pandora. "Is there something alive in the box? I am going to take just one peep, and then shut the lid as safely as ever. There cannot possibly be any harm in just one little peep!"

Meanwhile Epimetheus, who had been playing with other children, decided to return to Pandora. He stopped to gather some flowers—roses and lilies and orange blossoms—to make a wreath for Pandora. Epimetheus reached the cottage door and entered softly, for he meant to surprise Pandora. But just as he came in the door, Pandora had put her hand to the lid and was on the point of opening the box. If he had cried out, Pandora would probably have let the lid drop. But Epimetheus, although he had said very little about it, was just as curious as Pandora to find out what was in the box. And if there was anything pretty or valuable in it, he meant to take half of it for himself. So he was just as foolish and nearly as much to blame as Pandora.

There was a heavy peal of thunder outside, but Pandora did not notice. She lifted the lid and looked inside. It seemed as if a sudden swarm of winged creatures flew out of the box and brushed past her. Then she heard Epimetheus cry out, as if in pain.

"Oh, I am stung!" he exclaimed. "Naughty Pandora! Why have you opened this wicked box?"

Pandora let the lid fall and started over to see what had happened to Epimetheus. She heard a loud buzzing, as if a great many huge flies or mosquitoes were flying about. Soon, she was able to make out a crowd of ugly little shapes with wings like bats and terribly long stings in their tails. It was one of these that had stung Epimetheus, and before long, Pandora began to scream with pain. An ugly little monster had settled on her forehead and would have stung her badly, if Epimetheus had not run and brushed it away.

Little did the children know it, but these ugly things were the whole family of earthly troubles. There were evil tempers; there were a great many kinds of cares; there were more than a hundred and fifty sorrows; there were diseases in many painful shapes; there were more kinds of evil than it would be of any use to talk about. All the sorrows and worries that hurt people today had been shut up in the mysterious box and given to Epimetheus and Pandora to keep safely, so that the happy children in the world might not be troubled by them. Had they taken care of the box as they should have, no grownup would ever have been sad, nor any child have had cause to shed a single tear, from that hour until this moment.

Now the winged troubles flew out of the window and went all over the world. They made people so unhappy that no one smiled for many days afterward.

Meanwhile, Pandora and Epimetheus remained in the cottage. Epimetheus sat down in a corner with his back to Pandora. She rested her head on the box and cried bitterly.

Suddenly, there was a gentle tap on the inside of the lid.

"What can that be?" said Pandora, raising her head.

It sounded like the tiny knuckles of a fairy's hand, knocking lightly on the inside of the box.

"Who are you?" asked Pandora.

A soft voice spoke from within, "Only lift the lid, and you shall see."

"No, no," answered Pandora, "I have had enough of lifting the lid. There are plenty of your ugly brothers and sisters already flying about the world."

"Ah," said the voice again, "They are no brothers and sisters of mine. Come, come, my dear Pandora, I am sure you will let me out."

The voice sounded so kind and cheerful that Pandora and Epimetheus together lifted the lid. Out flew a bright, smiling, fairylike creature. She flew to Epimetheus and lightly touched the spot where the trouble had stung him, and at once the pain was gone. Then she kissed Pandora on the forehead, and her hurt, too, was cured.

"Pray, who are you, beautiful creature?" asked Pandora, gazing with wonder at the lovely fairy.

"I am to be called Hope," answered the sunshiny figure. "I was packed into the box that I might comfort people when the family of troubles got loose in the world."

"And will you stay with us," asked Epimetheus, "forever and ever?"

"As long as you live," said Hope, "I promise never to leave. Sometimes you will not be able to see me and you will think that I have gone away forever. But perhaps when you least dream of it, you shall see the glimmer of my wings on the ceiling of your cottage."

And ever since then, troubles have been flying about the world and making people suffer, but always Hope, the fairy with rainbow wings, has come to bring healing and comfort.

(Adapted from *A Wonder Book* by Nathaniel Hawthorne)

THE PYGMIES

Adapted from Nathaniel Hawthorne

A great while ago, when the world was full of wonders, there lived a million or more little people, who were called Pygmies and were no taller than six or eight inches. A whole family could fit into a shoe. They had little cities, with streets two or three feet wide, paved with the smallest pebbles, and bordered by homes about as big as a bird's cage. The Pygmies planted wheat and other kinds of grain, which, when they had grown and ripened, overshadowed these tiny people, just as a big oak tree overshadows you and me. If a stalk of wheat ever happened to come crashing down upon an unfortunate Pygmy, it was apt to be a very sad affair. If it did not smash him all to pieces, at least, it must have made the poor little fellow's head ache.

Now these funny Pygmies had a Giant named Antaeus for

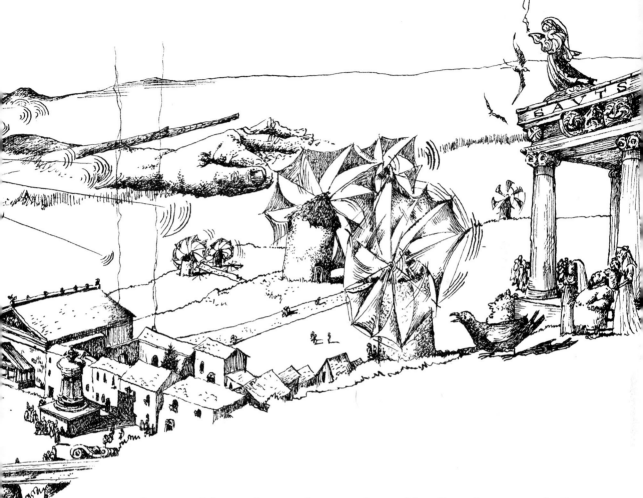

their neighbor, who was bigger, if possible, than they were little. He carried a pine tree, which was eight feet through the trunk, for a walking stick.

The Pygmies loved to talk with Antaeus; and fifty times a day, one or another of them would turn up his head, and shout through the hollow of his fists, "Halloo, brother Antaeus! How are you, my good fellow?" and when the small, distant squeak of the Pygmy voice reached his ear, the Giant would answer, "Pretty well, brother Pygmy, I thank you," in a thunderous roar that would have shaken down the walls of their strongest temple, only that it came from so far up.

He was always ready to do them any favor. For example, when they wanted a breeze to turn their windmills, the Giant would set all the sails going by merely pursing his lips and blowing. Antaeus loved the Pygmies, and the Pygmies loved Antaeus. Yet once, he sat down upon about five thousand Pygmies. But this was one of those unlucky accidents for which nobody is to blame, so the small folks never took it to heart, but requested the Giant to be careful where he squatted.

One day the mighty Antaeus was lolling at full length among his little friends. His head was in one part of the kingdom, and his feet extended across the boundaries of another part. The Pygmies scrambled over him, and peeped into his cavernous mouth, and played in his hair. Sometimes the Giant fell asleep, and snored like the rush of a whirlwind. During one of these little bits of slumber, a Pygmy chanced to see something, a long way off, which made him rub his eyes, and look sharper than before. At first he mistook it for a mountain and wondered how it had grown up so suddenly out of the earth. But soon he saw the mountain move. As it came nearer and nearer, what should it turn out to be but a human shape, not so big as Antaeus, it is true, although a very enormous figure.

The Pygmy scampered, as fast as his legs would carry him, to the Giant's ear, and stooping over its cavity, shouted lustily into it.

"Halloo, brother Antaeus! Get up this minute and take your pine tree walking stick in your hand. Here comes another Giant to have a fight with you."

"Poh, poh!" grumbled Antaeus, only half awake, "None of your nonsense, my little fellow! Don't you see I'm sleepy? There is not a Giant on earth for whom I would take the trouble to get up."

The stranger was coming directly towards Antaeus. Until there he was, with a golden helmet, polished breastplate, a sword by his side, a lion's skin over his back, and on his right shoulder he carried a club.

By this time, the whole nation of Pygmies had seen the new wonder, and a million of them set up a shout, all together.

"Get up, Antaeus! Up with you, lazy bones! The strange Giant's club is bigger than your own, his shoulders are broader, and we think him the stronger of the two."

Antaeus could not endure to have it said that anyone was half so mighty as himself. With this remark he sat up, saw the stranger, then leaped to his feet and thundered, "Who are you? And what do you want in my land?"

The stranger did not seem at all disturbed.

"What's your name?" roared Antaeus again. "Speak, or I'll bash your skull with my walking stick."

284

"You are a very discourteous Giant," answered the stranger, quietly, "and I shall probably have to teach you some manners before I leave. My name is Hercules. I come this way because this is a convenient road for my travels."

Then the Giant strode tower-like towards the stranger, and hurled a monstrous blow at him with his pine tree which Hercules caught upon his club; and being more skillful than Antaeus, he paid him back with such a rap upon the head that the great lumbering man-mountain tumbled flat upon the ground. The poor little Pygmies (who really never dreamed that anybody in the world was half so strong as their brother Antaeus) were a good

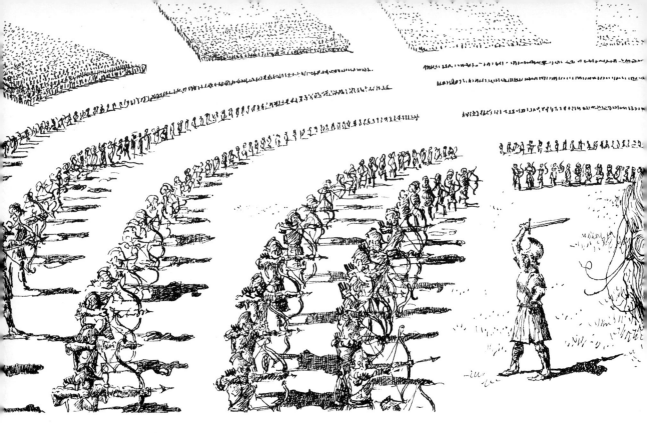

deal dismayed at this. But no sooner was the Giant down, than
up he bounced again. He aimed another blow at Hercules, but
missed, and his pine tree went deep into the ground and stuck
there.

Hercules put his club aside. "Step forward," he cried. "We'll
try which is the better man at a wrestling match."

"Aha! then I'll soon fix you," shouted the Giant; for, if there
was one thing on which he prided himself more than another, it
was his skill in wrestling. The two giants in rage hurled themselves
at each other. First Hercules fell to the ground, then Antaeus.
The impact of their bodies and the vibration of air completely
destroyed the Pygmies' capital city.

Hercules was wiser than this numbskull of a Giant, and had
thought of a way to win the fight. Watching his opportunity, as
the mad Giant made a rush at him, Hercules caught him around
the middle with both hands, lifted him high into the air, then
gave his huge body a toss, and flung it about a mile off, where it
fell heavily and lay with no more motion than a sand hill.

"Hercules has killed our enormous brother," cried the Pygmies.
Hercules took no notice, and perhaps thought the voices were
small birds that had been frightened from their nests. Now Hercules had traveled a long way, and was so weary after the fight,
he lay on the ground and fell fast asleep.

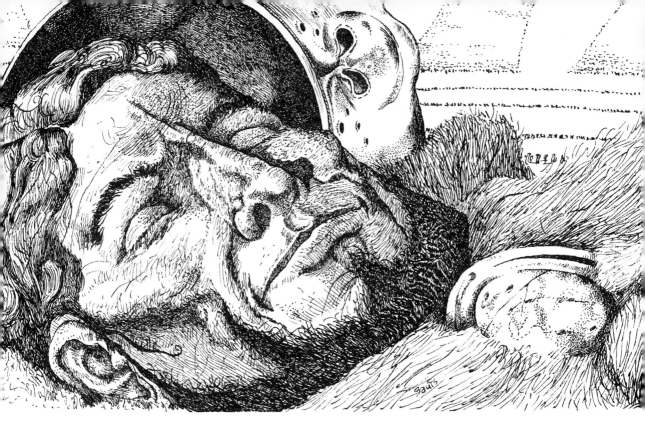

The whole nation of Pygmies decided to destroy Hercules before he awakened.

All the fighting men of the nation took their weapons, and went boldly up to Hercules, who still lay fast asleep. A body of twenty thousand archers marched in front, with their little bows all ready, and the arrows on the string.

The captains ordered their troops to collect sticks, straws, dry weeds, and whatever combustible stuff they could find, and make a pile of it, heaping it high around the head of Hercules. The archers were ordered to attack Hercules the instant that he stirred. Everything being in readiness, a torch was applied to the pile around Hercules' head, which immediately burst into flames.

But no sooner did Hercules begin to be scorched than he jumped up, with his hair in a red blaze of fire.

"What's all this?" he cried, bewildered with sleep.

At that moment the twenty thousand archers twanged their bowstrings, and the arrows came whizzing, like so many winged mosquitoes, right into the face of Hercules.

"Villain!" shouted all the Pygmies at once. "You have killed the Giant Antaeus, our great brother. We declare bloody war against you and will slay you on the spot."

Surprised at the shrill piping of so many little voices, Hercules, after putting out the fire in his hair, gazed all about, but could see nothing. At last, however, looking narrowly on the ground, he saw the numerous Pygmies at his feet. He stooped down, and taking up the nearest one between his thumb and finger, set him on the palm of his left hand, and held him at a proper distance for examination.

"What in the world, my little fellow," questioned Hercules, "can you be?"

"I am your enemy," answered the valiant Pygmy, in his mightiest squeak. "I challenge you to instant battle, on equal ground."

Hercules was so tickled with the Pygmy's big words and warlike gestures, that he burst into a great explosion of laughter, and almost dropped the poor little mite of a creature off the palm of his hand.

But Hercules was touched by the little man's courage, and could not help acknowledging such a brotherhood with him as one hero feels for another.

"My good little people," said he, "not for all the world would I do an intentional injury to such brave fellows as you! Your hearts seem to me so exceedingly great that, upon my honor, I marvel how your small bodies can contain them. I will leave you in peace. I will take five strides and be out of your kingdom at the sixth. Good-by. I shall step carefully for fear of treading upon some fifty of you, without knowing it."

He left them, one and all, within their own territory, where their descendants are alive to the present day, building their little houses, cultivating their little fields, spanking their little children, and reading their little histories of ancient times. In those histories, perhaps they read about their ancestors, of hundreds of years ago, and how they bravely stood up to the mighty Hercules and frightened him from their land for killing their friend, the Giant Antaeus.

(Adapted from *Tanglewood Tales* by Nathaniel Hawthorne.)

AN ECHO AND A FLOWER

Adapted from
a Greek Myth

Echo was a beautiful nymph who lived in a forest. She skipped and danced about the woods, up and down the hills and along the banks of riverlets and streams. Her beauty was so striking that she gave joy to everyone who looked at her. But joy soon vanished when she started to talk—because she didn't stop. She prattled aimlessly for hours and anyone in her company became so weary that even her beauty seemed to fade. Echo's incessant babbling so infuriated Juno, the goddess of the heavens, that she took away Echo's ability to speak her own words. All Echo could do was repeat the last two or three words that other people said. Sometimes she even made sounds that animals and birds made.

"Twit twoo," she sang when she heard a hoot owl.

"Croa-a-ak," she gurgled when she heard a toad.

"Honk, honk," she sounded when she heard a goose.

A monotonous life, indeed, for poor Echo, who was used to talking, talking, talking.

One day that started out to be a usual kind of a day in Echo's life turned out to be most UNusual. She saw before her in the woods, the most handsome man she had ever seen. This young man was a hunter, named Narcissus. "I must be seeing a vision," thought Echo. She clinched her fists and put them to her eyes and rubbed. Then she opened her eyes wide and looked again. He was still there.

"Oh, if only this handsome hunter would say some kind words that I might repeat them," she said to herself longingly.

Echo did not know that the handsome Narcissus was so in love with himself that he had little time for anyone. He moved forward. Echo followed, hiding behind one tree and then another. Narcissus heard her footsteps behind, turned and discovered her.

"Hello," Narcissus said.

"Hello," Echo repeated.

"Who are you?"

"Who are you?"

"Do you live nearby?"

"Do you live nearby?"

"Are you silly?"

"Are you silly?"

"Stop that!"

"Stop that!"

A few minutes of hearing himself repeated so disgusted Narcissus that he turned away and left her with nothing but a "Hrumph!" He found no time for Echo and her senseless imitations. Besides, he had himself to think about.

Echo turned away in tears. She knew she was defeated, and any attempts to win Narcissus would be hopeless.

Some say that the lovely nymph, Echo, was so grieved that she went up on a hill and turned to stone. Nothing was left of her but her voice, which to this day can be heard repeating the words of others.

In the meantime, Narcissus went his own way, thinking only of himself—with never a thought of any man, except when he was flattered or bestowed favors. The just gods of the heavens watched his actions and the fate of poor Echo. They decided he must be punished for his vanity. One day as he was out hunting, he came upon a quiet pool. He leaned down to quench his thirst, and he saw his reflection in the water. He smiled, and the face in the water smiled. The gods kept him at the pool admiring himself. Narcissus was spellbound by his reflection and could not leave. He lingered there for days, smiling and nodding at the water—even forgetting food and drink—until he finally wasted away. The gods came to take his body away to the land of the dead. In the place where Narcissus had been lying grew the beautiful Narcissus flower.

THE FLIGHT OF ICARUS

By Sally Benson

Once long ago in Greece there lived a famous mechanic named Daedalus. While visiting Crete, King Minos, the ruler of the island, became angry with him, and ordered him shut up in a high tower that faced the lonely sea. In time, with the help of his young son, Icarus, Daedalus managed to escape from the tower, only to find himself a prisoner on the island. Several times he tried by bribery to stow away on one of the vessels sailing from Crete, but King Minos kept strict watch over them and no ships were allowed to sail without being carefully searched.

Daedalus was an ingenious artist and was not discouraged by his failures. "Minos may control the land and sea," he said, "but he does not control the air. I will try that way."

He called his son Icarus to him and told the boy to gather up all the feathers he could find on the rocky shore. As thousands of gulls soared over the island, Icarus soon collected a huge pile of feathers. Daedalus then melted some wax and made a skeleton in the shape of a bird's wing. The smallest feathers he pressed into the soft wax, and the large ones he tied on with thread. Icarus played about on the beach happily while his father worked, chasing the feathers that blew away in the strong wind that swept the island. And sometimes he took bits of wax and worked it into strange shapes with his fingers.

It was fun making the wings. The sun shone on the bright feathers; the breezes ruffled them. When they were finished, Daedalus fastened them to his shoulders and found himself lifted upwards, where he hung poised in the air. Filled with excitement, he made another pair for his son. They were smaller than his own, but strong and beautiful.

Finally, one clear, wind-swept morning, the wings were finished, and Daedalus fastened them to Icarus's shoulders and taught him how to fly. He bade him watch the movements of the birds, how they soared and glided overhead. He pointed out the slow, graceful sweep of their wings as they beat the air steadily, without fluttering. Soon Icarus was sure that he, too, could fly, and, raising his arms up and down, skirted over the white sand and even out over the waves, letting his feet touch the snowy foam as the water thundered and broke over the sharp rocks.

Daedalus watched him proudly but with misgivings. He called Icarus to his side, and putting his arm around the boy's shoulders, said, "Icarus, my son, we are about to make our flight. No human being has ever traveled through the air before, and I want you to listen carefully to my instructions. Keep at a moderate height, for if you fly too low the fog and spray will clog your wings, and if you fly too high the heat will melt the wax that holds them together. Keep near me and you will be safe."

He kissed Icarus and fastened the wings more securely to his son's shoulders. Icarus, standing in the bright sun, the shining wings drooping gracefully from his shoulders, his golden hair wet with spray and his eyes bright and dark with excitement, looked like a lovely bird. Daedalus's eyes filled with tears and, turning away, he soared into the sky and called to Icarus to follow. From time to time, he looked back to see that the boy was safe and to note how he managed his wings in his flight. As they flew across the land to test their prowess before setting out across the dark wild sea, ploughmen below stopped their work and shepherds gazed in wonder, thinking Daedalus and Icarus were gods.

Father and son flew over Samos and Delos which lay to their left, and Lebinthus, which lay on their right. Icarus, beating his wings in joy, felt the thrill of the cool wind on his face and the clear air above and below him. He flew higher and higher up into the blue sky until he reached the clouds. His father saw him and called out in alarm. He tried to follow him, but he was heavier and his wings would not carry him.

Up and up Icarus soared, through the soft, moist clouds and out again toward the glorious sun. He was bewitched by a sense of freedom and beat his wings frantically, so that they would carry him higher and higher to heaven itself. The blazing sun beat down on the wings and softened the wax. Small feathers fell from the wings and floated softly down, warning Icarus to stay his flight and glide to earth. But the enchanted boy did not notice them until the sun became so hot that the largest feathers dropped off and he began to sink. Frantically he fluttered his arms, but no feathers remained to hold the air. He cried out to his father, but his voice was submerged in the blue waters of the sea, which has forever after been called by his name.

Daedalus, crazed by anxiety, called back to him, "Icarus! Icarus, my son, where are you?" At last he saw the feathers floating from the sky and soon his son plunged through the clouds into the sea. Daedalus hurried to save him, but it was too late. He gathered the boy in his arms and flew to land, the tips of his wings dragging in the water from the double burden they bore. Weeping bitterly, he buried his small son and called the land Icaria in his memory.

Then, with a flutter of wings, he once more took to the air, but the joy of his flight was gone and his victory over the air was bitter to him. He arrived safely in Sicily, where he built a temple to Apollo and hung up his wings as an offering to the god.

(From *Stories of the Gods and Heroes*)

Persephone

By Flora T. Cooke

Demeter had the care of all the plants, fruits, and grains in the world. She taught the people how to plow the fields and plant the seeds. She helped them gather in their harvests. They loved the kind Earth Mother and gladly obeyed her. They also loved her daughter, the beautiful Persephone.

Persephone wandered all day in the meadows among the flowers. Wherever she went, birds, singing merrily, flocked after her.

The people said, "Where Persephone is, there is the warm sunshine. Flowers bloom when she smiles. Listen to her voice: it is like a bird's song."

Demeter wished always to have her child near her. But one day Persephone went alone into a meadow near the sea. She made a wreath of delicate blossoms for her hair, and gathered all the flowers that her apron could hold.

Far away across the meadow she saw a white flower gleaming. She ran to it and found it was a narcissus, but far more beautiful than any she had ever seen. On a single stem were a hundred blossoms. She tried to pick it, but the stem would not break. With all her strength she grasped it, and slowly the narcissus came up by the roots.

It left a great opening in the earth which grew larger and larger. Soon Persephone heard a rumbling like thunder under her feet. Then she saw four black horses coming toward her from the opening. Behind them was a chariot made of gold and precious stones. In it sat a dark, stern man. It was Hades.

He had come up from his land of darkness, and was shading his eyes with his hands. In the sunny meadow Hades saw Persephone standing, beautiful with flowers. He reached out and

297

caught her in his arms, and placed her in the chariot beside him.

The flowers fell from her apron. "Oh, my lovely flowers!" she cried, "I have lost them all."

Then she saw the stern face of Hades. Frightened, she stretched out her hands to kind Apollo, who was driving his chariot in the sky overhead. She called to her Mother, Demeter, for help. No one answered her.

Hades drove straight toward his dark underground home. The horses seemed to fly. As they left the light, Hades tried to comfort Persephone. He told her of the wonders of his kingdom, of all the gold and silver and precious stones which he possessed. In the dim light, as they went along, Persephone saw gems glittering on every side, but she did not care for them, and she wept bitterly.

"I have been very lonely in my vast kingdom," said Hades. "I am bringing you to my palace, where you shall be my queen. You shall share all my riches with me."

But Persephone did not want to be a queen. She longed only for her mother and the bright sunshine and the sweet-smelling meadows.

Soon they came to the palace of Hades. It seemed very dark and dismal to Persephone, and very cold, too. A feast was ready for her, but she would not eat. She knew that anyone who ate in Hades' home could never again return to earth. She was very unhappy, though Hades tried in many ways to please her.

Everything on the earth was unhappy, too.

One by one the flowers hung their heads and said, "We cannot bloom, for Persephone has gone."

The trees dropped their leaves and moaned, "Persephone has gone, gone."

The birds flew away, calling, "We cannot sing, for Persephone has gone."

Demeter was more miserable than anyone else. She had heard Persephone call her, and had gone swiftly home to find her. She searched all the earth for her child.

She asked everyone she met on her way these questions, "Have you seen Persephone? Where is Persephone?"

The only answer she ever received was, "Gone, gone. Persephone is gone!"

Soon Demeter became a wrinkled old woman. No one would have known that she was the kind mother who had always smiled on the people. She sat mourning day and night, her great tears falling steadily upon the cold ground. Nothing grew upon the earth and all became dreary and barren.

It was useless for the people to plow the soil. It was useless to plant the seeds. Nothing could grow without the help of Demeter, and all the people were idle and sad.

Demeter wandered into many lands, and when she found no one on earth who could tell her about Persephone, she looked up toward the sky. There she saw Apollo in his bright chariot. He was not driving as high in the sky as he was wont to do. He had been hidden by dark mists so that no one had been able to see him for many days.

Demeter knew that he must know about Persephone, for he could see all things on earth and in the sky.

"O great Apollo," she cried, "pity me, and tell me where my child is hidden."

Then Apollo told Demeter that Hades had carried Persephone away and that she was with him in his underground home.

Demeter hastened to great Father Zeus, who could do all things. She asked him to send to Hades for her daughter. Zeus called Hermes. He bade him go as swiftly as the wind to the home of Hades.

Hermes gladly obeyed, and he whispered the joyful news to all he met on his way. "I am going for Persephone. I am going for Persephone. Be ready to welcome her back!"

He soon arrived in the gloomy kingdom under the earth. He gave Hades the message from Zeus. He told about the barren earth and of how Demeter was mourning for her child. He said she would not let anything grow until Persephone came back. "The people will starve if she does not soon return," he said.

Then Persephone wept bitterly, for that very day she had eaten a pomegranate and swallowed six of its seeds, and she remembered that whoever ate in Hades' home could never return to earth again.

But Hades took pity upon her and said, "Go, Persephone, back to the sunshine. But the law must be obeyed, and you shall come back every year to stay with me one month for each seed that you have eaten. That is all I ask."

Joy gave her wings, and as swiftly as Hermes himself, Persephone flew up into the sunshine.

Suddenly the flowers sprang up. The birds flocked together and sang; the trees put on bright green leaves. Everything, great and small, began to say in its own language, "Be happy, for Persephone has come! Persephone has come!"

Demeter was so benumbed with sorrow that she did not at once heed these voices. But soon she saw the great changes all about her and was puzzled. "Can the earth be ungrateful? Does it so soon forget my sweet Persephone?" she cried.

It was not long, however, before her own face grew radiant. She became once more the kind Earth Mother, for she held again her beloved child in her arms.

When Demeter found that Persephone could stay with her only half the year, she brought out the choicest treasures from the storehouse, and while Persephone stayed, the world was filled with beauty and joy.

When she had gone, Demeter carefully covered the rivers and lakes, and spread a soft white blanket over the sleeping earth.

(From *Nature Myths and Stories*)

Illustration Acknowledgments

The publishers of *Childcraft* gratefully acknowledge the following artists, photographers, publishers, agencies, and corporations for illustrations in this volume. Page numbers refer to two-page spreads. The words *"(left),"* *"(center),"* *"(top),"* *"(bottom),"* and *"(right),"* indicate position on the spread. All illustrations are the exclusive property of the publishers of *Childcraft* unless names are marked with an asterisk (*).

1: Robert Keys
6-9: Janet Palmer
10-14: Robert Byrd
15-17: Jerry Pinkney
18-25: Erik Blegvad after Hugh Lofting
26-33: Robert Lawson *
34-35: sculpture, Suzi Hawes; photo, Frank Cassidy
36-37: *(left)* U.S. Department of Agriculture *; *(center)* Donald W. Nusbaum, *The Milwaukee Journal *; (right)* Walter Chandoha *
38-45: photo, Ylla, Rapho Guillumette *; art, Richard Keane
46-51: Ernest H. Shephard *
52-53: art, Mary Hauge; *Childcraft* photo by John Gajda
54-59: Mary Hauge
60-61: art, Mary Hauge; photo, George Silk, *Life* © Time Inc. *
62-63: Ewing Galloway *
64-65: Russ Kinne, Photo Researchers *
66-67: George Suyeoka
68-71: Gyo Fujikawa
72-73: Clark Bruorton
74-75: *(left)* Clark Bruorton; *(right)* Frank Cassidy
76-77: Ed Emberley
78-79: Leo Lionni
80-81: Gordon Laite
82-83: art, Clark Bruorton; photos, *(left)* Photo-Library *; *(right)* Gerard, Monkmeyer *
84-85: Robert Borja
86-91: Kinuko Craft
92-93: Byron Davies
94-97: Lois Axeman
98-103: Ilse Bischoff
104-105: art, Franz Altschuler; photo, Thomas Peters Lake *
106-107: Franz Altschuler
108-109: German Tourist Information Office *
110-115: art, Susan Perl; photo, Conzett & Huber *
116-121: Franz Altschuler
122-123: *(left)* Franz Altschuler; *(right)* Frank Cassidy
124-130: Georges Michel
131-139: Jerry Pinkney
140-141: Hope Taylor

142-143: Nicolas Sidjakov
144-149: William Pène du Bois
150-153: sculpture, Suzie Hawes; photo, Frank Cassidy
156-157: *Harpers Weekly* *
158-159: sculpture, Suzi Hawes; photo, Frank Cassidy
160-165: photo, Al Werthmann, Shostal *; art, Bill Rhodes
166-171: Ingri and Edgar Parin d'Aulaire
172-185: Mary Horton
186-189: Lynd Ward
190-201: George Suyeoka
202-205: Mary Hauge
206-207: *(left)* Mary Hauge; *(right)* Frank Cassidy
208-211: George Suyeoka
212-219: Leonard Weisgard
220-225: Brian Wildsmith
226-233: Victor Ing
234-235: Bill Rhodes
236-245: art, Clark Bruorton; photos, *(pages 236, 239, 244)* Frank Fenner, *(pages 236-237 center)* Eric Schaal *, *(pages 238, 245)* Kaufmann & Fabry *, *(pages 238-243)* H. Armstrong Roberts *
246-251: Jerry Pinkney
252-257: Marcia Brown
258-261: Victor Ambrus
262-267: Tom Feelings
268-269: Ralph Creasman
270-271: *(left)* Ralph Creasman; *(right)* Frank Cassidy
272-275: Stephen Antonakos
276-281: Robert Lostutter
282-289: William Albert Sauts Bock, Jr.
290-291: Museo Nazionale, Rome (Art Reference Bureau) *
292-295: wood engraving by Brussel-Smith, © Hercules Incorporated *
296-301: Charles Mikolaycak

Heritage binding cover—*(left to right): (back)* Ilse Bischoff, Brian Wildsmith, Marcia Brown, James Lewicki; *(spine)* Victor Ambrus, *(front)* Feodor Rojankovsky, Brussel-Smith, © Hercules Inc.*, Kinuko Craft, Ed Emberley

Author Index

Use this index to find a story if you know the name of the author. If you know only the title, use the index on page 304. In addition, the General Index in Volume 15 is a key to all the books.

Title Index

Use this index to find a story if you know the title. If you know only the name of the author, use the index on page 303. In addition, the General Index in Volume 15 is a key to all the books.